A Single Woman's Guide to Raising a Healthy and Productive
Young Man, Based on the Wisdom of the Book of Proverbs

RAISING
AND
LOVING
HIM

TONYA MOLTON

RAISING AND LOVING HIM
A SINGLE WOMAN'S GUIDE TO RAISING A HEALTHY
AND PRODUCTIVE YOUNG MAN, BASED ON THE
WISDOM OF THE BOOK OF PROVERBS

iUniverse books may be ordered through booksellers or by contacting:

iUniverse
1663 Liberty Drive
Bloomington, IN 47403
www.iuniverse.com
1-800-Authors (1-800-288-4677)

Because of the dynamic nature of the Internet, any web addresses or links contained in this book may have changed since publication and may no longer be valid. The views expressed in this work are solely those of the author and do not necessarily reflect the views of the publisher, and the publisher hereby disclaims any responsibility for them.

Any people depicted in stock imagery provided by Getty Images are models, and such images are being used for illustrative purposes only.
Certain stock imagery © Getty Images.

ISBN: 978-1-5320-7296-3 (sc)
ISBN: 978-1-5320-7295-6 (e)

Library of Congress Control Number: 2019907588

Print information available on the last page.

iUniverse rev. date: 06/14/2019

DEDICATION & PRAYER

Proverbs 16:3 (NLT)
Commit your work to the Lord, and then your plans will succeed.

God,
Thank you for allowing this blessing. I pray that this book be a
light of encouragement and of hope, in Jesus name. Amen.

This book is dedicated to the sunshine in my life, my two grandson's
Ely (9 years old) & Emari (7 years old)! I love you both with all my
heart! And to my entire family who are so important to me!

Last, but not least to the one who holds my heart, thank you for
loving and believing in me! Always my love! No matter what!

Tonya and son Eric

My grandsons Ely and Emari

CONTENTS

INTRODUCTION IX

Chapter 1 WORDS FROM THE HEART 1
Chapter 2 MUCH LOVE 4
Chapter 3 HEAR ME. 7
Chapter 4 FEEL ME 9
Chapter 5 MY LIGHT. 11
Chapter 6 KNOW ME 14
Chapter 7 RESPECT ME 15
Chapter 8 LOVE ME. 16
Chapter 9 SUPPORT ME. 17
Chapter 10 WORDS FOR LIFE 19
Chapter 11 PATHWAY FOR LIFE 30
Chapter 12 LESS THAN THE BEST DECISION. 34
Chapter 13 MOTIVATION. 40
Chapter 14 FINANCE. 43
Chapter 15 KEYS TO SUCCESSFUL BUDGETING. 49
Chapter 16 CREDIT. 54
Chapter 17 BANKING 58
Chapter 18 BUYING A HOME 60
Chapter 19 STOCKS, INVESTMENTS, and RETIREMENT 72

BOOKS REFERENCES 77

INTRODUCTION

Proverbs 8:1-6 (NLT)

Listen as wisdom calls out! Hear as understanding raises her voice! She stands on the hilltop and at the crossroads. At the entrance to the city, at the city gates, she cries aloud, "I call to you, to all of you! I am raising my voice to all people. How naïve you are! Let me give you common sense. O foolish ones, let me give you understanding. Listen to me! For I have excellent things to tell you …

I remember like it was yesterday: the birth of my son Eric, my only child. I can hear his cry just as vividly as the day that he blessed my life with his grand entrance into the world, but now a husband and father with a family of his own I couldn't be more proud of him. I still feel that he is a blessing in and to my life. I honor the man in him and respect the husband and father that he has found his way to become.

Ladies, we have to properly equip our young boys with the right tools to allow them to move through life proudly and enable them to connect to love.

There are certain things that hold our young men down; some are gender-specific and some are race-specific. Some things that our young boys go through in life other young boys of another race don't go through, or if they do, they don't always experience it to the same degree because of economic background or a missing parent.

As the head of the home we must first build a solid ground on which we can stand and hold our heads up high. I am talking about building self-esteem, great character, and morals by knowing who you are and whose you are. You need to know and believe that you are children of the Most High God, and through Him you can do and be anything! You need to take a stand in your life, because if you don't stand for something you will fall for anything. That's one thing that I know for sure because I have hit the ground plenty of times through this journey called "my life." I truly believe, Ladies, that you want nothing less than the very best for yourself and your children. We all do!

Ladies, we need to find the right tools to place us on the right path to help catapult our lives to the next level of self-wholeness, and the book of Proverbs gives you the solid foundation that you and I have been searching for. Hear me out! Don't give up on me yet! If you want to thrive in life, don't discount what can be a total blessing to you and your family. It's better to build your house on solid ground; anything less is treacherous sand.

Ladies, sit back, relax, and free your mind and let's start off with a little exercise to help you remember what it's like to be a child, think about your younger days when you were in your formative years. Think about all of the things that you loved as a child, things that made you happy, things that made you smile. Take the time to remember the things that made you feel good inside, like your mother tucking you into bed at night—maybe she gave you a kiss on your forehead before saying, "I love you." Or perhaps hearing the words "I am so proud of you" made you feel good.

Also reflect back on all of the things that pulled you down, things that made you sad, that didn't make you feel good about yourself. You didn't like it when someone called you a "stupid, dumb jacka—," or said, "You are just like your no-good daddy. I can't stand to look at you." Those things didn't feel good to you as a child, did they? Well, guess what? They don't to our kids, either. We are breaking our boys down every day by not knowing that what we place inside them as children will carry over into their adult lives and will affect their abilities to make good, sound decisions.

Emasculate is defined as to castrate; take away virility; to soften; vitiate.

Ladies, consider this definition every time you feel the need to vent on our young men; then take a new stand.

Proverbs 15:13 (NLT)
A glad heart makes a happy face; a broken heart crushes the spirit.

Ladies, let's build a man by raising a man, not by tearing him down."

Proverbs 10:21 (NLT)
The godly give good advice, but fools are destroyed by their lack of common sense.

CHAPTER 1

WORDS FROM THE HEART

It's nothing like the real thing, but sometimes in order to allow hope to float, a substitute will do. When you sit down and really talk to most men to find out why they feel and act the way they do, you normally get the same response: "There wasn't a male in my household to show me how to be a man and what to do." The truth is, the majority of our young men are being raised by young, single women, mothers not just in their mid-to-late twenties, but in their early teens as well. These young girls are rearing our young males, and that's making things even harder for our young boys, because nine times out of ten the young mothers are trying their best to make adult decisions when they are but children themselves. This does a great disservice to our young men, but it does not have to be to their detriment.

I know, because that was me thirty-five years ago. I had my son out of wedlock at the tender age of nineteen. His father was around for a minute, but after things went bad between us, then that old saying rang true: "Mama's baby and daddy's maybe." I was left all alone, trying to raise a son whose father had abandoned him physically and emotionally, just because we weren't a couple anymore. But I have to give him credit because he did pay child support, but his visits with his son were limited and few. Let me make this clear: it's not about my son's father—it's about my journey of being a single mother—so there is no shame here because he did more than most. What I did appreciate about him was that whenever he did come around, he was always positive and loving towards his son and respectful to me.

In raising my son, I was a child trying to raise a child. I thought I was making good, sound, adult decisions, but what I was actually doing was making the best decisions I could with the situation and the ability that was in me at the time.

Ladies, keep in mind that this book isn't intended to beat you down into the ground but to give you a helping hand by sharing my life experiences as a single mother rearing a male child alone. This is my way of sharing my love and support by letting you know that you are not alone.

I was nervous about my son's future and the future of the family he would eventually begin, so I actually sat down and mapped out a plan for his life. I know that sounds silly, but I had to do something in order for my baby boy to stand half a chance in the world. I'm not one who thinks, *the world owes me anything*, but I realize that our young men don't always have an equal advantage. I decided that I wouldn't allow my son to use that as an excuse for failure or to not give life his best shot!

The playing field isn't always at the same advantage when playing the same game of life. Even playing on the same field they might have some bad curveballs pitched to them and, society may embrace each male differently. Some may get one bad ball tossed to them, and if it happens to be a strike, the game is automatically over in most cases. There is no strike two and three! I really don't know why this is the reality for some young men, but it is, so we have to find a way to safeguard our young boys. It all starts with the rearing of our boys, and that starts with the decisions that we as mothers make early on.

Proverbs 4:25-27 (NLT)
Look straight ahead, and fix your eyes on what lies before you. Mark out a straight path for your feet; then stick to the path and stay safe. Don't get sidetracked; keep your feet from following evil.

True, I have made many mistakes along the way—and we all have and will—but because of God's grace and His mercy, my son and I weathered through right on up to his adulthood. I can truly say that God has been merciful and good to me.

Even though this section of the book is directed towards my Ladies, it is about our baby boys! I wrote it for the person who will most likely to be the one who will mold our boys and keep him protected until manhood, the one who had his back from day one—and that's you, my sister! You don't get enough recognition for the selfless love you give and the struggles that you go through in rearing our young boys. I know you normally only hear about our boys being in trouble and that it's all because of being raised by a single mother, and it's hurtful. We could easily point the finger at absent fathers, but then there would be three fingers pointed back at you and me.

There are two sides to every story: the side of the person who is telling the story and the side of the person who hasn't had a chance to tell his or her side. A close friend pointed out that obviously people are going to believe the side of the person who told the story first, but that doesn't necessarily make the story true.

You are hearing the story from a woman's point of view, but this is not about the slicing and dicing of the missing parent. The reality of it is nothing matters more to me than saving the lives of our young boys! Ladies, let's unite with our men to become a strong front for the sake of our future and our families.

Ladies, remember this: if you take one step, I'll take the next one. I am here for you, my Ladies, and you are definitely not alone. If you don't believe anything else, please believe that *you can do all things through Christ Jesus, who strengthens you!* (Phil. 4:13.) My God is here for you because he believes in you. He would not give you more than you can bear.

CHAPTER 2

MUCH LOVE

Proverbs 22:6 (NLT)
Teach your children to choose the right path, and when they are older, they will remain upon it.

Raising a male child is so different from raising a female child. I am very passionate about our young men and the success of their lives. I am not talking about financial success, but being healthy and whole in mind, body, and spirit. Anyone who really knows me knows that I have a tender spot in my heart for our young men and that I deeply care for their well-being.

So often our young boys are left to fend for themselves because of circumstances beyond their control. I know that things are hard, but you can't give up! I won't let you give up! Things may not be fair, but it's up to you to make things right when it comes to your life. Don't depend on daddy, because he's not there, and don't harbor deep feelings because of his absences. It's only going to hurt you in the long run. He's gone on with his life, and you are still carrying around the hurt and pain. Stop it! No more! That's one dream you should allow to die, or you will die a slow death trying to hold onto the possibility of *"what if"*! Don't allow anyone to cancel out the dream that's buried deep inside of you that hasn't had a chance to be birthed. It's unfortunate that someone else in your life made a personal decision that will affect your childhood and your adulthood, but you still have a great and wonderful life ahead of you that was planned by God Almighty. Think about your family and your future.

God is going to place the right wife in your life to love, care, and respect the man that you are. You are no different from anyone else. You have a bright future, but you just can't see it for the clouds that have accumulated over your head. If you allow yourself to rise above those clouds, you will see that the sun is still shining! Those clouds are just an illusion, and they are blocking your view of the real picture! Just don't give up.

Your beginning doesn't determine your end; if that were the case, I wouldn't be here writing this book just for you. I didn't make the best decisions in my youth, but had I listened to society, I wouldn't have made it this far. The odds were stacked against me because I was black and a teenage mother, but I decided I needed to get into the driver's seat if I wanted to take control of my life. Yes, being a young black female and pregnant statistically may have been negative, but those factors didn't have to be harmful to me! There is an old saying, *'Against all odds,'* and *that's what you have to believe and say, 'I'm going to make it against all odds!'* You can do this!

Back to you, ladies! First of all, we must believe in what we can't see and that's called faith. The future is what's to be, but no one knows what it holds; we must believe that whatever it holds is worth fighting for.

Proverbs 18:22 (NLT)
The man who finds a wife finds a treasure and receives favor from the Lord.

Ladies, it says nothing about going out to look for a man, but it does speak to us about being a virtuous woman. A virtuous woman has a lot of great attributes that will attract her husband because it's not all about the physical.

You see, the physical is fine, but what about the mind? I can understand our young men when they say they want someone who is capable and able to make good, sound decisions in life—a helpmate that actually meets the definition of a helpmate.

Let's get real. Some of us are more of a *"hurt-mate"* than a helpmate! Come on now! Don't get mad—let's get real. Don't get me wrong; there's nothing wrong with taking care of yourself, but, we need to *take care* of ourselves! Get me? Yes, it's OK to look good, because men are visual creatures, but they want someone with some substance to add to that glamour-girl look. Your looks can only take you so far. I am not judging! Remember, I am here with you and on your side, but we have to really believe what we have is worth more than rubies and is precious and special. It says so in the Bible:

Proverbs 31:10-12 (NLT)
Who can find a virtuous and capable wife? She is worth more than precious rubies. Her husband can trust her, and she will greatly enrich his life. She will not hinder him but help him all her life.

Our bodies are temples and should be treated as such. There is an old adage: *"Why buy the cow when the milk is free?"* Ladies, that is why so many of us are still single, raising our young boys on our own, and it is partially why our men are absent from the home. We didn't hold our men accountable for doing right by us. They "hit it and quit it," and we were still holding on, just like our young boys!

Ladies, I have been there before—more times than you know—but I had to start loving myself in order to love my son. I couldn't have every Tom, Dick, and Harry stopping by to see me just because I was lonely and in need of a little TLC.

I made a decision early on that I wouldn't have different men over my son. Kids tend to mimic what they see. Their little brains are like sponges absorbing everything in reach. They are constantly aware of their surroundings. Believe me they know what's going on in your life and in your bedroom. You may think that you are keeping it on the down-low with Joe, but our little boys really do know! They are always taking a mental video of your life and storing it in their memory banks to help them sort out their lives later. So, if your life is a revolving door, with different men coming and going, then our boys will grow up to be men who think that that's how life is; they will think, *My mama allowed it, so it must be OK.*

Ladies, as Matthew 7:6 says, "Do not give what is holy to dogs ..." (NASB). He will only do what a dog knows best, which is to run from place to place sniffing and marking his territory. Don't allow a man to run back and forth, in and out of your life, using you at his convenience then leaving behind our most precious possession, and our future leaders. Our young boys deserve better. I am not preaching to the choir; I am standing alongside you, singing those old familiar songs. Listen, I've gone through it all. I should be singing lead or even my own solo. All I am saying to you, my Ladies, is stand and be strong. Build your house on solid ground because anything else is shifting, treacherous sand. A house will never stand without a solid foundation.

Sex before marriage is like building your house on quicksand; eventually it will cave in. If a brother really wants you, he doesn't mind investing quality time getting to know you. If he is really serious about you and respects the quality woman you are, he will wait until marriage to make love to you. Ladies, it's so important that our young men see your life in a positive light in their formative years. They are sensing how a lady should be treated by the way the men in your lives treat you.

General Information

- *Men will only do to you what you allow them to do.*
- *Build a solid relationship before moving on to the next step.*
- *Be a good example for our boys.*
- *Don't allow men to treat you as a revolving door.*
- *Respect yourself, and others will, too.*
- *Work on your inner beauty.*
- *Let a man seek you.*

CHAPTER 3

HEAR ME

When my son was three or four years old, I met a young man. This young man appeared to be very nice and sweet. He was very polite and gentlemanly, but my son didn't take to him. Every time my son saw him, he would tell him the same thing: "You better not kiss my mom or my dad is going to beat you up." His action struck me as odd. That wasn't like my son at all! I was puzzled by his behavior, but it made me pay close attention to this young man. It seemed as though my son felt the need to protect me, even at such an early age. I couldn't figure out why he felt that way. As time went on, my son continued to try to assert himself as the man of the house every time this particular person came over. Now, mind you, I had male friends who were really just my friends. (Don't try to read this as a secret code for "boyfriends!" I know it's easy to think, *Oh, the old "he's just a friend" thing*, but trust me …) My son didn't react that way with any of my male friends. Eventually I found out that this brother had a fiancée and was engaged the entire time he was seeing me! The perfect gentleman—or so I thought—had every intention of walking down that aisle with his fiancée, but he felt no need to share that bit of important information with me. My son picked up on his deception from day one. Believe it or not, children have a better sense of true sincerity in people.

Ladies, I know that you are probably saying, "She is crazy. I would have spanked his behind for being disrespectful," but here is the deal: there were several things going on in that situation. Primarily, I recognized that the conduct wasn't my son's normally obedient behavior, so that raised a red flag for me. It heightened my awareness of my surroundings when it came to this particular relationship. I paid closer attention to my son's concerns, and I validated him as a person. He had a concern but didn't know exactly how to express it clearly. The best way he felt to get my attention was to act out of character.

Ladies, sometimes when our kids are having a fit about something, let's not jump so quickly to put them back in their place. My main concern as a mother was my son's well-being. I validated my son by asking him questions about this young man, and he said in so many words that he didn't like him. I told the young man that I could no longer see him. Of course, he tried to pretend that he was so hurt about the split, but I knew better. And after all, he was engaged the entire time we were seeing one another. My son picked up on his deception, but I didn't. I am not saying that every time your child throws a fit you should drop your companion, but get to know your son's temperament, and if it changes drastically or if he acts uncomfortable when someone is around, then you may need to be concerned.

Don't discount your child's feeling just because he's a kid or because you just have to have a man. A lot of our boys are being mistreated and abused by the men that we allow to walk in and out of our lives. When those abusive men leave, they may be gone, but they leave behind broken or damaged spirits. The sad thing about it is that our little boys are trying to send out warning signals the best way they know how, but we are missing them because sometimes love is blind and desperate, and our boys end up paying for our bad judgment.

At a very early age, our young boys try to establish who they are as people. When the adult male is absent from the home, our boys tend to want to step up into the position of being the man of the house. That's why they get so cocky early on, because instinctively the man's position is to lead the family, and if the son is the only male in the house, then what? Yes, he's going to be the one to try to protect his family. That's why you see a lot of our boys on the street slinging dope. When you talk to these young men about why they are on the corners, the answer almost every time is, "I got to help put food on the table and clothes on my family's backs." Ladies, let's not put our young boys in this position by making them carry such a heavy burden.

Proverbs 10:2 (NLT)
Ill-gotten gain has no lasting value, but right living can save your life.

Mirror Moments

- *We need to validate our boys' concerns at a young age.*
- *Don't be so quick to discount your son's feelings.*
- *Don't be so quick to break him down by spanking him.*
- *Start talking to your children maturely when they are young.*
- *Know your child's behavior patterns.*

CHAPTER 4

FEEL ME

I was at a local grocery store one day, and there was a young couple shopping. They had two kids, a little boy and a girl. The little boy was in a shopping cart that was made like a race car, and the little girl was walking beside her mother. The couple appeared to be in their late teens or early twenties. I was attempting to go around the young mother, but she didn't notice because her back was turned to me. Her male companion saw that I was trying to get by. I heard him say, "Man, move you're a— out of the way; that lady is trying to get by." She turned around and smiled and said, "I'm sorry."

I continued to shop, and then proceeded to the checkout. I noticed that the couple was checking out ahead of me in another lane. When I got outside I saw the couple again as I walked to my car. They had parked on the same aisle, across from my car. The mother was placing the groceries in the car, and her companion was pushing the little boy in the race car shopping cart down to the cart return area. The little boy didn't want to get out of the cart because he had enjoyed the ride. All of a sudden I heard a loud smack, and the mother turned and calmly asked, "Why did you hit him?" The young brother slung her son out of the cart by one arm.

Without hesitation he replied, "His a— wouldn't get out of the cart! I don't have time for his sh—." To the boy he said, "Nigga, I don't care about your crying! I will leave your black a— here. Don't make me leave you're a— here! I ain't your daddy!" The young mother turned and continued to load the car, never once validating or standing up for her son while he was being broken down into a million pieces.

Ladies, here are my concerns: *first*, I was concerned with the disrespect of the young mother in the store and the fact that she did not stand up for herself. *Second*, she allowed her son to see her being disrespected. Remember, he was taking a mental video of his surroundings and storing it in his memory bank for later reference. The *third* thing is she allowed her son to be mentally and physically abused by this young brother and never spoke up for him. If you could have seen the look in that little boy's eyes as he looked around crying out for his mother's help! We are the only voice our kids have, and if we don't stand up for them, then who will?

Mirror Moments

- *Don't stand or sit around allowing our boys to be abused.*
- *Only permit men of good character into your—and your child's—life.*
- *Don't put up with the least disrespect.*
- *Never allow someone to call your child names.*
- *Remember, often your voice is the only voice your child has.*

CHAPTER 5

MY LIGHT

When my son was in the third or fourth grade, I remember dropping him off at school and being met by his teacher, who told me that the school counselor wanted to see me. After being directed to the counselor's office to inquire why she needed to speak with me, I was advised of the good news concerning my son. The counselor explained that the school had tested my son to see if he had been abused or mistreated in any way, and the results were great!

He was asked to draw a picture to represent his home life and surroundings. He drew a picture that showed happiness, unity, and love.

The counselor talked about the good news for a long time; I allowed her to finish her every word. I smiled and kept my mouth closed until she was finished. Finally, I asked her why my son was tested and why it was done without my consent. If there had been any concerns, why wasn't I contacted?

She replied that his teacher had recommended it because my son always looked down or away when someone was talking to him. Had I been asked, I could have answered that question within two seconds: my son was shy and never made eye contact with anyone he interacted with. But instead of mentioning it to me first, his teacher had taken it upon herself to have him tested for abuse. Normally, I wouldn't have minded, but in this case I felt that his teacher was being nasty because she and I had had an exchange of words before.

The teacher had once approached me as I walked my son to his classroom. She rudely stated that she thought I was doing my child's homework for him each night. I replied, "My son does his own homework. I sit with him every night and go over it with him."

"I know his penmanship," she said, "and he's not writing his homework—you are!" I was agitated because I knew that I didn't do my son's homework for him, but if I did, how dare she question me?

"Are you calling me a liar?" I asked in a stern voice.

"I know his penmanship, and he's not doing his homework," she repeated.

By this time I was really upset, but I never raised my voice because my son was still standing beside me holding my hand. My final remark to her before I kissed my son good-bye and headed down to the principal's office was, "I make sure my son takes his time to write everything nice and neat. If I can't read it, then he has to rewrite it. Since you have over twenty students in your class, you don't have the same time to invest one-on-one in his writing as I do." Here is the deal: because I was a young, black, single mother, she prejudged and assumed that my boy couldn't be as smart as he was—and as respectful, too. I had to be wrong, so she had him psychologically tested which he passed. I was told when he had to draw his home life he drew a happy and positive picture.

There were a couple of things going on in this situation. *First*, she didn't realize that she was dealing with a parent who was very positively active in her son's life. *Second*, I didn't allow her to pull me out of the realm, or light, that my son was used to seeing me in, but I was able to stand my ground and defend the integrity of my son. *Third*, I validated my son's capabilities as a student by standing up for him. *Fourth*, because she had a problem with me, she took it out on my son; she tried to get to me by using the fact that my son was shy and had a timid personality. Her little scheme backfired on her. She had no right to test him without my consent, so I reported her to the principal again. Ladies, don't get indignant, but do be assertive when it comes to your child's future.

Had the teacher taken the time to ask me why my son never looked anyone in the eye, I would have told her that his grandmother on his father's side was very shy. She was a very loving, kind, and gentle woman, and would stand and talk to you for three hours and never look your way. From the time he was three months old until he turned four, my son's grandmother kept him for me while I was at work. That was part of his formative years, and he picked up on her behavior.

Had his teacher asked me why he never looked anyone in the eye, she would have learned that I was personally working with my son to fix this habit whenever I caught him looking away while interacting with others. Whenever I saw my son looking away, I would take the palms of both of my hands and gently cup his chin towards the person talking to him, or I would say in a soft voice, "Baby, look up when someone is talking to you." I would also explain the reason and the importance of why he should look someone in the eye. Never once did I jump down his throat, calling him crazy and making him feel disrespected or belittled—and neither did I allow anyone else to! One family member tried to joke about his downcast eyes by making a negative comment—"Is he crazy?"—and laughing at him. I addressed the problem right then without a smile on my face. I advised that person that I wasn't going to allow anyone to disrespect my son by calling him names, even if it was just a joke. Children's hearts are like little nets holding onto what they've captured from others' actions and comments.

I always addressed my son when I caught him looking the other way. Now my son has a habit of staring directly at you while you are talking to him, and he holds his head at the same angle that I used to hold it when I would catch him looking away when someone was speaking to him. I don't care who is speaking to my son—he will look them straight in the eye without blinking.

Mirror Moments

- *Never allow anyone to deliberately belittle your child.*
- *Stand up for your child's rights, even when you are being challenged.*
- *Don't allow anyone to pull you out of character.*
- *Be active in your child's life.*
- *Never overlook important issues that affect your child.*
- *Be visible and involved when it comes to your child's education.*

CHAPTER 6

KNOW ME

Ladies, I want to share with you the importance of this topic for our young boy's development. We tend to think that between the ages of about two and six all our young boys need is a truck to play with and a small tree to climb, but the truth is they need direction. Those years are when they are learning and trying to figure out things. Why do you think you see them on the floor taking things apart? We normally get upset and want to spank their butts because we consider this action destructive and feel that they are breaking the toys, when in reality they are just trying to figure out how things work. It's sort of like going outside to find your husband with your car jacked up and him underneath it, working on only God knows what, and you wanting to scream because he's not a mechanic. But tinkering is a part of manhood, so don't get mad. It's their instinct just like mothering is a little girl's.

It is so important that we make a positive connection with our boys at a young age. We really need to start enforcing or setting general rules when they are two years old or younger. They need boundaries and limitations, or you will have a misbehaving child later in life. I think that boys are harder to control when they get out of hand, so it's important to catch them early on.

CHAPTER 7

RESPECT ME

Never allow anyone to call your son stupid, dumb, crazy, ignorant, or anything that is degrading in your presence without addressing it. I am not saying you should get into an argument every time someone makes a statement you don't agree with, but stand up and make it clear that you don't allow anyone to disrespect your child. Everyone—no matter how young—should be respected and deserves respect! I'll share with you the reason why! Even though your child may never tell you, name-calling hurts him, and he will carry that hurt in his heart and mind well into his adulthood. Those types of scars run deep beneath the surface and are hard to see but sometimes very easy to mask.

Did you pick up on how my son's experience with his grandmother affected his growth? I didn't see it as a negative because they both were shy, but society did see it as a negative, so I had to gently nudge him out of his shyness. We grow from our experiences in life. Yes, some people do overcome their past, but some people struggle every day because of words that were said to them in childhood. You can't protect your children from every single derogatory thing in the world, but it is your duty as a parent to shield and protect them from what you are able. Everyone has baggage in life, but what we don't want is for our young men to have an entire luggage set to tote around. Remember, it's about our boys and the protecting and building of their future.

Remember, this is not an attack on you. I am right here with you, and I have gone through many of the same struggles, too. I have made lots of mistakes, but I want to save you the heartache and pain by sharing my journey with you! My hat is off to you, because we wear many of the hats. You should always walk with dignity with your head lifted high. You are a true survivor! No matter what negative things you have been confronted with, just know that no one knows your walk like someone that has walked the same path.

CHAPTER 8

LOVE ME

Let's continue! There are some things that we need to start working on, now that we have established that our boys need to see and feel positive interaction in their lives. There is another very important and key element that I purposely failed to mention previously, and that is the TLC that our boys need. They are human like everyone else. They need to be hugged, loved, and tucked in at night. I know you don't want to make your sons soft, but would you rather him grow up to be coldhearted and callous? Believe it or not, your sons will tell you when you have given one kiss too many or one hug over the limit, but they still need to be kissed and hugged to feel loved and good about themselves. It's better for him to let you know that you have given too much loving than for him to not receive any at all. Take a trip down Memory Lane and look back on when he was a baby and how you used to dote on him by kissing his cheeks or blowing on his stomach or just rubbing his body down with baby lotion. He would just smile and laugh! He was taking in all of your good loving, and he felt your love, too! So why stop? Everybody needs to be touched and made to feel special—even you! Why is he any different?

Love is so important in our lives, love help turns the center of who we are. You find that most people who were raised in a loving environment with a loving family tend to excel in life and are able to cope better when things don't go as planned. They also are able to bounce back or roll with the punches much easier than someone who didn't get to experience the love of someone special in their life.

Love covers a multitude of things even our short comings. Remember we all have them, but loving who you are helps us to move around our shorting comings easier. When you love who you are you tend to exude self confidence, and feel secure about who you are and are willing to take chances on yourself. You make better life decisions and tend to stand up for yourself because you see yourself in a brighter light. Ladies love is the key and the way

CHAPTER 9

SUPPORT ME

I remember walking my son to his second-grade class and holding his hand as I had done ever since he had been in kindergarten. On this particular day, I remember him dropping my hand as we approached his class. I didn't think anything of it; I grabbed his hand again. Again he released my hand, but this time he turned to me and said, "Mom, you can't keep holding my hand."

I was sick to my stomach—talk about a wounded heart! This was my child! Every night I would go to his room, tuck him in, give him a kiss, and tell him, "I love you," but I had to back off because he was trying to stand on his own and become independent. Can you believe a second-grader wanting space and showing independence? Ladies, the icing on the cake that day was when my son also told me that he no longer needed me to walk him to class. But here is the key that turned his heart towards me: I respected him as a person, put a bandage on my wounded heart, and backed away slowly. I still got out of my car with him in the mornings, but I only walked him as far as the hallway of his classroom. Oh yeah! I had to get a quick kiss in the car, too, but only if none of his friends were around.

See, my son still wanted his hugs and kisses in private, but in public he wanted everyone to see him as a big boy. I stood back and accepted his decision—fighting my feelings every inch of the way—because I was open to my son's maturity process. My son felt validated, and it made our bond even tighter. Guess what? Later on, in his late teens, he returned to wanting to hold my hand and cuddling up next to me when we talked. He wanted me at his football games and band competitions and wanted to show outward emotion towards me in public. There's nothing better than when God blesses your relationship between you and your teenager. While other parents were sharing with me their horror stories, I was telling them about the goodness of God's mercy and glory in my relationship with my son and me.

Mirror Moments

- *Allow God to direct your path.*
- *Your son needs love to grow into a healthy and productive male.*
- *It's OK to kiss and hug your son at a very young age.*
- *Allow your son to discover who he is and his place in life.*
- *Be supportive during his stages of development.*
- *Your son's surroundings and his interaction with others play a key role in his formative years.*

CHAPTER 10

WORDS FOR LIFE

Here are some things that we must keep on hand at all times to use in the development of our young men. Never allow any of these qualities to stray away from your reach because they are key pieces to our boys' development in life.

Integrity—Wholeness; completeness; honesty; uprightness (Webster Dictionary)

At a very young age we must instill in our boys the importance of their integrity and the role that it plays in life: it's the cornerstone of a healthy mind. Your integrity states a lot about you. When you have a child who constantly wants to have his way no matter what—even if he has to cheat or throw tantrums to get his way—you have to nip that in the bud early on, because what you are allowing to form is a troubled child and/or teenager. Ladies, the Bible says that if you spare the rod, then you spoil the child (Prov. 13:24). And that statement is so true; even though you have heard it over and over, those words are worth a million dollars in raising a healthy, young male. Ladies, I am not giving you a green light to beat your child until your arm gets tired, but I am saying to correct your child when he needs it. You can't jump on every little thing he does, but do not allow him to continue to play with matches until he burns down your house. When you start early with positive enforcements, it helps to develop and form your son's integrity, or self.

Dignity—Nobility of the mind and character; worth (Webster Dictionary)

Ladies, do you see how both words in this list so far are closely related to the same thing: the character of a person? Not only is it important that we treat our young boys with dignity and respect, but we must teach them that they must treat others with respect and dignity. My favorite statement in life is the Golden Rule, "Do unto others as you would have them do unto you" (Matt. 7:12). Those words are so powerful! There is no proverb that says, "You must respect me even if I am disrespectful and mean to everyone I interact with." I can tell you that ain't happening, because life is a circle and what you do will catch back up to you, and no matter how hard you try to run from it, it will catch you. Most people who have problems with people disrespecting them are individuals who do not respect others or who appear to be very timid! Either way, we must work on both of those areas if they are present in our young boys' lives.

Love—To feel devotedly attached to or affectionate toward; to feel strong tenderness and passion for; to like; take pleasure in (Webster Dictionary)

Love is so important in the development of our young boys. This particular emotion is where our passion comes from. In order for us to pursue things with a whole heart, we must have passion. When we are passionate about something, we tend to go after it at all costs. For example, most boys love sports, and they are aware of the risk of injury to their little growing bodies, but they don't care because there's a certain burning deep down inside. They have already counted the cost, but they are willing to spend whatever it takes because of their passion. Most boys instinctively love and enjoy the sport itself, but if the passion isn't there, more than likely they won't excel. We really need to start cultivating our young boys for manhood, and, believe it or not, love plays a major role in all of our lives—not just our boys'.

Love gives a feeling of security, respect, and worth! So here's another key to help prepare our little ones for life: we need to touch the inner core of who they are. We also need to share with them our hearts; give them love; build trust and unity; and teach them the Golden Rule, "Do unto others as you would have them do unto you." (In a nutshell, look at how you want to be treated and respected as a person, and give that to your son ten times; boys and young men need to feel respected.)

This subject was mentioned earlier, but it was worth repeating because it's so important! I pray that you really get this part! Listen to your heart before reacting to your flesh (no name-calling), and be intimate with your son (*everyone* needs to feel important and special). Everybody responds in a positive way when they feel loved and cherished. However, it's a fine line between being loved and respected and being spoiled! Please don't cross over the line! Spoiling a child is like fueling a raging fire; nothing is ever enough! There is no need to buy his love. Your love is necessary and very important to your son's growth and development because he can never give what he's never received. The way your young boy feels about himself and how he interacts with the one he loves has a lot to do with how he will respect others and cope in society. Usually if he has no respect for his mother, other people that are close to him, or the law, then he will have no respect for anyone else. We need to teach respect to our young boys at a very young age, because it has a great deal to do with how he perceives the world and how the world receives and views him. (See "**Respect**," below.)

Independence—*Freedom; lack of restraint or dependence; income sufficient to free one from reliance on others (Webster Dictionary)*

Boys tend to reach for their independence a lot sooner than our little girls, but boys mature more slowly than girls! I am not talking about "I'm grown and I am moving out" independence; I mean that our boys tend to want to start doing things on their own and in their own way. As women, we might think that they are being rebellious, but they are only gravitating towards what's natural.

My nephews, Malik age seven and R.J. ten, came to stay with me for six weeks one summer. I sat back and watched the two interact with one another. I wanted to see which was the more timid of the two and which demanded more attention. Malik was OK with me giving him a bath, but R.J. wouldn't have it. So when it came time for R.J's bath, instead of helping him bathe I would go over the list of things I wanted to make sure he washed, like under his arms, his face, his neck, his private parts, his feet, his hair, etc. Without fail, he would respond, "I know, Auntie. I know what to do." The older one was more independent than the younger one in that particular area, but I noticed that the younger one loved to get his own drinks and food, while the older one didn't mind me waiting on him hand and foot! The younger one wanted my attention constantly and would do things to bring attention to him, and the older one would sit back and take everything in. Malik asked questions about how to do things, but R.J. just tried to do it on his own, even if it took him twenty minutes to figure it out. This is an example of how boys value their independence, but can show it in different ways. Our sons' independence is so important, but they pick and choose what they want to be independent of. Ladies, just bear with your sons walking two feet in front of you in public and wanting to give you hugs and kisses only in secret. Remember, they are trying to establish who they are and where they fit in.

Respect—*To esteem; regard with deference (Webster Dictionary)*

I personally think that love and respect go hand –in hand. To me they are very closely knitted together. I have already discussed how important love is in the development of our young men; respect is right there with love. I love that old saying, "You don't have to like me as long as you respect me!" I agree with it to an extent. I believe that true respect comes from love, but some people believe that you can respect somebody and not even like them. I don't know if I agree with that opinion. I personally think that in that case the person is being phony or forced to endure the other person's presence, maybe because of social status or the role that the other person plays in their life. Here's a good example: an acquaintance once told me that she hated a certain individual and that the only reason why she had anything to do with that particular person was because of her status, the role that the other person played in her life. She only tolerated the other person's presences because she was forced too! That simply blew my mind, because if you saw her interact with the person she said she hated, you would have never known that she harbored such deep resentment towards the other, unsuspecting person. She was being phony and was putting up a front towards the person she said that she hated. That's why I say love and respect are coupled together in the same package. I believe that we must really work hard to build a good, solid foundation based on love and respect; both of these two areas help turn the key to a healthy life. If you respect and love yourself, then you will be able to love another and show respect to someone else without being phony. Loving you helps build self-esteem. It allows you to follow your passion or calling in life, and love allows you to feel and feel the hearts of others.

Support—*To sustain; to hold up; to provide for; pay living expense; to substantiate; verify; to champion; advocate; to endure; to bear; to prop (Webster Dictionary)*

Support is so important in the growth of our young men! I can't begin to tell you how important it is to them to know that someone "has their backs!" Ladies, our boys hang out on the corner with other young boys because of the support that they give to each other. I've heard our young boys say, "That's my dawg. Man, I'll die for him. I know he got my back!" What he really means is, "My boy supports what I'm doing—even if it's running drugs, my boy encourages me in the way I handle things, and he's not beating me down into the ground with negative words." Yeah!

We may also hear, "What's up Dawg ?" I don't agree with the statement but he thinks that it's a far cry from you or another adult constantly telling him, "You ain't sh— and you will never be sh—. You're just like your father!" Guess what? You chose his father—he didn't—so when you feel the need to break your son down and toss his dignity into the trash, remember he's only reacting to your actions. Ladies, let's encourage our young boys. Give them hope even when things look hopeless. Romans 4:17 says, "… call things that are not as though they were" (NIV). Speak to those mountains in life, and they must move; teach our boys to do the same thing. Start encouraging them when they are young. Let them know that you have their back when the world turns its back to them and has them glued to the wall. I am telling you, your encouragement will make the difference between life and death to a growing young man trying to find his way.

Ladies, it is also important for our young men to have a positive male figure to look up to. If the father isn't in the household, then the next person in line is your mate, so, you really have to be careful about whom you choose to share your life with, because it affects your child's life, too! There are certain signs that we may misread or miss altogether, while another male might pick up on them within minutes. Don't allow the street to holla at our young men and our young men to holla back because they feel that's where they are receiving their love, support, encouragement, and respect. Support is the key to his heart!

Encourage—*To inspire; cheer; foster; promote (Webster Dictionary)*

Support and encouragement are a perfect team, to me, just like love and respect. All the things that I am mentioning are in some way tied together in the developmental process or growth of our young boys. I remember when my son was on the junior varsity football team, I would go to his games on Thursday nights to watch him play. Sometimes I would be there for a while, sitting back and watching him, before I would call out to him. Once my son looked up into the stands and saw that I was there, he would perk up and step it up a notch. Every time he ran the ball, I would stand up and yell, "That's my boy!" Even though he said I embarrassed him, he loved every minute of it; I saw it in the way that he moved when I cheered him on. Everyone likes encouragement—even grown men do. I have heard of situations in which men who had been married for years left their wives because they felt like their wives stopped being in their "corner" and no longer encouraged them. I don't agree with this, but it's a reality. The men said that they turned to someone new because that person encouraged and supported them and their dreams, that leaving their wives had nothing to do with the way the "other" women looked but how the women made them feel. This is our reality, but it shouldn't be an excuse. True encouragement is fuel to the soul!

Courage—*Bravery; mettle; fearlessness (Webster Dictionary)*

The word "courage" looks similar to "encouragement"—and one derives from the other—but the two are different in some ways. Courage is what gives you the green light to move forward. So many people are fearful of the "what-ifs" in life that they can't move forward. Courage isn't anything that someone else can give to you; it's something that comes from within. When dealing with encouragement, you have to wait for the other person to move, but courage is all about the move *you* make! If you never take a step, then you will never get anywhere, so stop being fearful. God didn't give you a spirit of fear, but of a sound mind (2 Tim. 1:7). Trust in God and have the courage to believe that you can do all things. When my son was little and he wanted to learn how to ride his bike without training wheels, he was nervous about getting hurt—but he knew that the only way to learn was to just do it! We removed the training wheels from his bike, and he mustered up the strength to get on that bike without the assistance of training wheels. He fell down and skinned his top lip, but he got back on that bike, and eventually he was able to ride without the wheels. He got past the "what-ifs" and did it! That took courage.

Confidence—*Trust; faith; belief in one's competence; assurance (Webster Dictionary)*

Confidence and courage are like a set of twins: they look so much alike, but they are separate individuals. When you have confidence in yourself, you are unstoppable. Ladies, I am talking to you, to me, and to anyone who will take the time to listen. Confidence will take you where nothing else will. You don't have to be the smartest or the brightest, but as long as you are confident, it will allow you to excel. Confidence is built and not instinctively received. Ladies, I can't stress to you enough how essential it is to build confidence in our boys. I am not advising you to always tell him what he wants to hear but to point out his strengths and don't be so quick to point out his weaknesses. Let him know that you are proud of the way he handles certain things. Build his house, his castle, on solid ground with an airtight foundation called "confidence." It's another very important tool in life that he can't afford to leave home without.

Proverbs 9:9 (KJV)
Give instruction to a wise man, and he will be yet wiser; teach a just man, and he will increase in learning.

Intimacy—*Close friendship or association; comradeship; sexual relation (Webster Dictionary)*

"Intimacy"— listen to that word! It sounds so darn sexy and smooth! You just want to say it over and over again! *Intimacy* … Or better yet, "into-me-see"—see what's in me, get to know me, let's relate by having relations! It's so important that you build relationships with your sons—it's the only way they will truly know how to relate to a woman. Our boys watch how others treat the women in their lives and mimic or mirror what they see. It's so important to carefully choose whom you allow to be part of your life, because they will have an influence on your impressionable son, and they don't even know it.

We all want to feel that warm, gushy feeling of being in love and intimate with our partners and not caring about what anyone else thinks. Your personal life is, after all, yours to do with as you please. But keep in mind that your life intertwines with your child's life, and it affects his life—not indirectly, but *directly*—so choose wisely. Also, your son needs to be intimate with you—not in a sexual way, of course—but he needs to feel your touch, your hugs, your kisses, and your sweet nothings whispered in his ear before he'll know the soft voice of another woman. It's just like how a little girl needs her father to open doors for her, buy her flowers, take her out to dinner, show her a special time, and tell her what a valuable jewel she is. Share your love with your son. I promise it won't make him soft; it will help create a compassionate, loving man and a great husband.

Psalm 111:4b (KJV)
The Lord is gracious and full of compassion.

Intimidate—To deter through fear; terrorize; frighten; browbeat (Webster Dictionary)

Looking at this word, it appears that it's closely related to "intimacy," but its meaning is very different. The word "intimidate" brings to mind something cold, harsh, and hard. The feeling you get from this word is nothing like the feeling you get from the word "intimacy." Intimidation is like an ice barrier that's blocking your view. You can see where you are trying to go, but the view is distorted and blurred. Your picture, or perception, isn't clear. When you are intimidated by something, it paralyzes you, preventing you from making a move in life. Nothing good in life is easy; you have to work hard and take a chance when things in life seem to be working against you. If you never take a chance in life, you will never know if you can achieve your dream. The Bible says that a just man falls down seven times, and every time he gets back up (Prov. 24:16).

Don't let fear of the unknown keep you from your destiny and dream. Intimidation will only intimidate you if you allow it to! I was intimidated for years when it came to speaking in front of people, because I am a fast talker. It's pretty bad when you confuse yourself by speaking too fast. My mind would be moving from neutral to first gear, but my mouth would already be in third gear, talking about something I had no control of. I knew what I wanted to say, but my mouth didn't give my brain enough time to gather my thoughts clearly; because I spoke so fast, it came out totally different! Sometimes I had to just stop and pause for several minutes until I gathered my words, and even then there was no guarantee that what I said would make sense and anyone would understand a word of it. I was afraid that others would judge me or misunderstand the point that I was trying to get across, so I wouldn't say anything.

I finally received the love of God and the spirit of the Holy Ghost and was delivered from that fear of speech. Now, I try to pay closer attention to my speech when interacting with others and being able to read their faces of confusion has helped me tremendously. I still talk fast, but I don't allow that paralyzing fear to take control of what God has in store for me to do. I just keep moving, praying for strength to endure, and I pray that what I've shared has made complete sense. Fear is only an emotion. You have complete control of your emotions, don't let intimidation (which is rooted in fear) intimidate you.

Proverbs 24:16 (KJV)
For a just man falleth seven times, and riseth up again.

Fear—*Dread; apprehension; alarm; anxiety; solicitude; worry; awe; respect; reverence*
(Webster Dictionary)

Fear and intimidation go hand in hand; they are like peanut butter and jelly. The two are the dynamic duo of doom. When one tags you, the other one is waiting in the wings, ready to jump in and make its move. Don't allow either of the two to invade your space, your mind, or your time. Your thoughts sit in the driver's seat of your car in life. If you allow either one of the dynamic duo of doom to become a passenger in your car, you may as well get ready to have system problems because of the negative magnetic force they bring along with them. Here are two positive forces to keep in mind to help protect you from the dynamic duo of doom: *don't fear,* and *trust in the Lord!*

Proverbs 3:25–26 (KJV)
Be not afraid of sudden fear, neither of the desolation of the wicked, when it cometh. For the Lord shall be thy confidence, and shall keep thy foot from being taken.

Words for Life

- *Integrity*
- *Dignity*
- *Love*
- *Independence*
- *Respect*
- *Support*
- *Encourage*
- *Courage*
- *Confidence*
- *Intimacy*
- *Intimidate*
- *Fear*

Proverbs 29:25 (NASB)
The fear of man brings a snare, but he who trusts in the Lord will be exalted.

These things are so important in getting to the core of raising a successful young man. I can't emphasize enough that certain tools in life play a key role in our development. Those twelve words may seem to be such a small list in the total list of words in our vocabulary, but they are the main keys to a very healthy human being. I suggest that you get to know them and their meaning! Remember when you were a student and your teacher gave you a weekly vocabulary list of words to study, and then you would be required to use them in a sentence to make sure that you truly understood the meaning? I ask that you use your twelve words the same way, but put them to use in your life instead. Build your confidence, find the courage to step out, fear less, and love more. Intimidate intimidation! Ladies, these words are for you and your baby boy, too!

Proverbs 14: 1 (NLT)
A wise woman builds her house …

As time goes on, things in your son's life begin to change. His child's body begins to form into a man's. Your little one may grow several inches in one summer, and his voice and his attitude may change. He begins to search for himself by looking for others who look like him, talk like him, walk like him …yes, another male. Teen years can be a blessing or a burden to a single parent. I like to call this stage, The Three *T*s of a Teen: test, trial, and terror—I mean, error!

Sister, this is the time that you really need to pray for patience, understanding, and remembrance, because you will be tested and placed on trial, and your son will make plenty of errors. You need to pray for patience, because he will continually stand on your last worn-out and very thin nerve. He will test you to see how far he can go, but hold on and stand firm; believe it or not, teens love rules even when they complain about having to follow them. If you have been streamlining his behavior and enforcing rules prior to his teen years, then you should be able to weather this storm without having to use a life preserver. I know when the fire is turned up and the heat gets hot, normally you would hear, "If you can't stand the heat, then get out of the kitchen." Well, your kitchen is a part of your house, and if it burns down, the house is dysfunctional. I say get out your fire extinguisher and put the fire out. A little bit of smoke damage is a far cry from your kitchen being totally destroyed! Ladies, he's worth the minor heartache you may have to endure to love him back into place. Remember when you were a teen and nobody could tell you anything either, Ms. Know-It-All, but look at you now, all grown-up with the shoe on the other foot!

Here are some things to do to keep his mind occupied and alive:

- Be active in his life.
- Go to his sporting events.
- Go to his school events.
- Challenge his thoughts on life.
- Find a common ground.

- Find a positive male to help him cope (a "Big Brother," etc.).
- Reassure him that you love him.
- Encourage him.
- Make a big deal about something positive he has done.
- Be the light that shines in his life; where there is light there is life, and where there is darkness you see no hope.

Males love trophies, encouragement, and for someone to believe in them. Start making him a scrapbook of all of his achievements. When my son graduated, I made the biggest stink about his graduation. I reserved a room at a local restaurant for his graduation dinner party. I made formal invitations on my computer announcing his graduation and his party. I explained how it would be an honor for guests to share with me my son's personal accomplishment. I made the day of his party a big deal and all about him! I made sure that everybody received a poem that I had personally written to my son telling him how special he was to me and how blessed I've been since he became part of my life. I decorated the main table with his trophies of accomplishments and with two huge poster boards displaying his pictures from birth to his graduation. One poster board contained many of his "firsts": his first haircut (his hair in a tiny bag), his first plane ride (the picture and ticket), his first trip to the White House (picture), his first school dance (picture), his first paycheck stub and the picture of him getting ready to go to work on his first day, and a picture of his first love (little old me). Everything was labeled and had a brief story connected to it!

The other poster contained photos of special moments and events throughout the years that were near and dear to his heart. Just like the other poster board, it contained very special things contributing to his journey through life up until that moment! I had pictures of him playing baseball as a kid, at band competition, on the field playing football, at senior prom, etc. If you could have seen the expression on his face when he walked over to the table, it was as though he had just been given a million dollars. My son stood there looking at those pictures as though he had never seen them before! Forget about the huge gift basket that I had, full of nicely-wrapped goodies and with a huge bow on it! He went straight to the poster boards, as did everybody else! I put together a complete program for this event. I placed programs for everybody next to the place settings. I made sure that everyone had a small gift and a thank-you note from my son as an appreciative gesture for coming out to help celebrate his accomplishment. Since God is the center of my life, I started off by thanking God for the blessing he had given to me and for allowing me to have such a special person in my life. Then I followed up by reading a passage from the Bible (Proverbs) concerning a child and his parent. Ladies, I love the book of Proverbs—I love the wisdom and great teaching that it contains!

It took such a small amount of my time to put together a lifetime of memories for my son! My son is now twenty-one years old, and he hasn't forgotten that occasion. The other day he came home from work with an award for good service (an article written about him and his work ethics), and he asked if I could keep it for him. His words to me were, "I know that you are going to put it together for me in something special!" And without another thought he continued talking about how his day had gone! But he was right! I made about twenty copies and handed them out to some of my family members and made sure that I talked about it to anyone who would listen, especially while he was around.

Ladies, that's not bragging about your child! It's called encouraging your child! There is a difference! You know how to get on the phone and tell anyone who will listen about how no-good he is when things are not going right or if he made a bad decision. (At least he made a decision! Some grown people are not able to make a decision at all.) Why not share with everyone his accomplishments in life, too? Boys love it when they know that they have made you proud. Even our men love it when we boast about them, because everyone loves to be important, adored, and looked up to! Why wouldn't our growing young men feel the same way, too?

CHAPTER 11

PATHWAY FOR LIFE

Our young boys also need the proper tools in hand to help them obtain a job! I think it's safe for me to say that we need to start directing our boys towards legitimate employment when they are between the ages of fourteen and sixteen. The first thing you need to do is to help your son create a résumé for himself, even if he's never been employed. A résumé shows that he's taking his job hunt seriously, and it gives his future employer a better idea of who he really is. Our boys need a leg up over the other candidates, and walking into a potential workplace with a résumé in hand is key and, I might add, very impressive for a teenager. This may seem a little extreme, but we have to go to the extreme to get our boys employed and off of the streets!

My son applied for his second job with a résumé I put together for him. The company he was submitting an application to hired him on the spot, and he stayed there for four years. My friends dogged me about my son being only sixteen years old and having a résumé with such little job history. But here's the deal: his résumé still contained a lot of important information about him and his capabilities. True, his job history wasn't long, but his interests were impressive, and so were his extracurricular school activities.

Your résumé contains more than just your job history; it gives your education, interests, goals, skills, and your main objective. There are so many different ways to put together a résumé. You can make a general résumé and list all of your jobs, or if you have worked in several different fields, you can put together a résumé that highlights certain skill in those fields. In today's world of technology and computers, the tools for creating the perfect résumés are at your fingertips. Most computers are already installed with software that has résumé templates; all you have to do is plug in your information. The only thing about that is your selection is limited, but you still have other options, such as buying the résumé software you prefer, getting a book on how to write a résumé, or having your résumé created professionally.

Things That You May Find on a Résumé

Your name, address and phone number—On most resumes you will find this information somewhere at the top.

Example:

John Doe
1414 Makebelieve Lane
No city, No state 11111
(P) 911-911-9999

Objective—This is very important when putting together your résumé. This is where you need to state what you are trying to accomplish by applying for a job with that particular company. In a nutshell, it's your personal mission statement upfront.

Example: *To obtain a key position with a progressive company that will allow me to excel by fully utilizing my skills and abilities in customer services.*

Job experience—This is the place to sell yourself and your time to shine. Act like a car salesman and point out in detail everything about your job and your duties; be very descriptive. Begin by listing your current position and end with your first job, or cover ten years of your employment history.

Example: If you were a hostess and now applying for a job in customer service, you would spice up the wording of the description of what your duties were. *I have six months of public relations, direct contact with customers, customer service, and assisting customers with inquires, and follow-up.*

Education—This is where you list all of your education, even Continuing Education courses.
List the highest level of education back to high school. List any other formal schooling that's pertinent.

Skills—Your skills are what you do or what you've done before. It's your experience highlighted for display!

Example: *Typing, writing, answering phones, customer service, accounting, driving, etc.*

Special interests/hobbies—This area is for things that you may volunteer to do in your spare time, things that you find interesting or things that you do personally for yourself.

Example: *Working with cancer patients, football, running track, sky diving, collecting ants, etc.*

Your résumé is your personal blueprint of your job experience. The sample I've provided isn't written in stone, but it's a stepping-stone to place your foot on. It's good to have a leg up above the rest.

Now that you have put together a résumé for your young son, you need to polish him for the job interview. This process is easy and simple. Here are some tips for you to give him:

- Make sure you make direct eye contact.
- Speak up.
- Ask questions if necessary.
- Be yourself and sell your qualifications and skills.
- Pay close attention to the person who is interviewing you, and answer the questions asked.
- Give a firm handshake.
- Dress to impress.
- Do not have gum or candy in your mouth while interviewing.

Some people get nervous when it comes to interviewing. Remember, you are in the driver's seat of everything that you do in life, and you have complete control! And always remember, God didn't give you the spirit of fear, but of a sound mind (2 Tim. 1:7).

Proverbs 13:14a (KJV)
The law of the wise is a fountain of life.

We also need to start grooming our young men for higher education. This is another avenue that we need to help prepare them to travel down. Our young men should start preparing for college while they are in middle school and junior high. College isn't for everyone, but it's worth exploring. There are many opportunities for our young men to prepare for higher education. First, your son should meet with his school counselor to make sure that he is taking the proper courses to prepare him for college. There are several subjects that are mandatory in order to get accepted into college. A minimum grade point average must be maintained. Make sure that he is making the grades. Don't just take his word for it. You need to take part in this process. He needs your assistance along with his counselor's assistance to help him through this process, to help him secure financial aid (scholarships, awards, or any other kind of programs that he may be eligible for) and to help him choose which college is best suited for him. Higher education is very important. Please, try to encourage your sons down this path, because their odds of succeeding in life will be greatly enhanced by doing so!

Mirror Moments

- *Start concentrating on higher education in middle school to high school.*
- *Keep up with his grades.*
- *Make sure he maintains a solid GPA.*
- *Work closely with his guidance counselor.*
- *Help him to apply for scholarship awards.*
- *Get assistance for any type of financial aid and grants.*
- *Make sure you work closely with his counselor to prepare the college applications.*

CHAPTER 12

LESS THAN THE BEST DECISION

Sometimes our young boys make some less-than-perfect decisions in life and end up on the wrong side of the law because of lack of direction, lack of experience, or peer pressure. We still must encourage them but not allow them to use their mistakes and your concerns as a crutch in life. It's OK to fall down in the sand, as long as we don't lie there until the sand turns to mud. It's easier to wipe off sand and keep on going, but it's harder to get mud off without some kind of assistance. Remember, to a certain degree we all have to make decisions for ourselves in order to mature, so, Ladies, if he makes a mistake that lands him in jail, don't panic. But if he ends up there a second time, then there is a problem, and you must nip that in the bud ASAP!

I am in no way condoning a boy going to jail, but this does occur—that's why I have taken my time to write this book. What I am saying is there's still hope for our boys! *Society has labeled them as a lost cause, a danger, or a menace to society—lazy and unproductive!* That's not true. Our boys do the same thing as other young boys growing up, but the difference is that for other boys society turns the other cheek and excuses their wrongs as minor mistakes or bumps in the road. Normally, their indiscretions are excused: "He's just being a teenager," and "He'll grow out of it; he's experimenting," or "He's just trying to find himself, and it's OK to give him a second chance." But our boys get the book slammed on them for the same offenses. Our boys receive excuses, too, but they are not of encouragement and second chances!

Since life isn't fair, we must play with the hand that's given to us until we are able to pick up a better deck of cards! I am not putting one race down to build up another, but life viewed and life lived are two different things. I'm speaking as someone who has lived the experience! And because I have lived through the experience, the window that I am looking out of is clearer than the window of the person who's looking through the same window from the opposite side. People who look from the outside never get to see the entire picture. Their view or take on what's really going on is limited. They can only see the room in which the window is located, but the complete house is much bigger than that one room!

I have found that it's very hard for our boys and men to get jobs once they have a criminal record, and it's even harder if the record contains a felony. It's funny how decisions you make as a child with a child's mind affect a great deal of your adult life. Don't wallow in self-pity; pick up your bed and start moving! After all, your decisions landed you where you are! Don't let your circumstances be your circumference in life. Sometimes circumstances place you in certain economic situations, but don't let that predict how you approach life. Listen, ladies, I know it sometimes gets hard with the bills, the kids, and life itself. And we sometimes relay those pressures to our young boys. Our teenage boys begin to feel like they have to step up and step out to help bring balance to the situation, and they end up making the wrong choice and sometimes end up serving time.

I am not saying this is the situation every single time, but nine times out of ten the reason our boys look to the street is to help resolve their economic situation, or because they're looking for love and affection! If, you find yourself on this side of the road, there is help and hope for you and our young boys. We still have time to get them on the right track! Look at Judge Mathis! He is living proof that it can be done, so, don't give up! As you may know, Judge Mathis was a juvenile delinquent, and he turned his life around by going to law school, then becoming a judge. Ladies, let's take some of the pressure off of you, because just like there are two sides to a coin, there are two sides to this matter. Here's the heads of your coin: *your son has to want to turn things around and change for the better!* Tails: *he needs your support and love to get through it!* At this point he must want to do right by himself, you, and society! Don't allow him to give excuses, because excuses will have you on a city bus headed to nowhere fast! An excuse is a shield used to avoid admitting your fault or guilt. The only shield that's necessary is the shield of faith. Encourage your son to believe in himself, and he will reach heights that only God could elevate him to! Every mother wants the best for her child, and I know that you are no different. Next, I want to share with you some tips that can possibly help our young men get back on the right track once they have been on the wrong side of the law.

First thing, Ladies: there is nothing better than a mother's prayer. Stay on your knees before God, asking for guidance and protection for your child. Many of our young men have been saved this way. Make God the head of your life!

Mirror Moments

- *Make sure that your son stays in contact with his probation officer.*
- *Make sure that your son's probation officer has your son's up-to-date address and phone number.*
- *Make sure he meets his curfews or restrictions.*
- *Ensure that he completes all of his volunteer work, community time, etc.*

- *Make sure that all of the fees are paid to his probation officer, as well as other related fees, and that all classes are completed.*
- *See if he can get his record sealed (so that the charge won't show up later).*
- *If he has a public defender or attorney, stay in contact with him or her.*
- *Share your concerns about the decisions made by your son's attorney on his behalf.*
- *Remain humble and positive.*
- *Know the guidelines that you have to follow.*

Most of this effort is really the responsibility of the boys themselves. Men, you must follow up and make sure that these things are completed, and don't just solely depend on your mother's help!

Ladies, make a game plan with your son—pull him over to the sideline and let him know that the game is not over. Just like in football when the team is behind and the coach pulls the team over to reevaluate the game plan, adjust and make changes so that he can see what is necessary to come out on top! Life is the same way: we must stop, reevaluate the situation, readjust, and move on to victory—even if it means the game has to go into overtime!

Mirror Moments

- *Talk to your son about his mistake.*
- *Make a game plan for how both of you can correct the mistake.*
- *Explain that this cannot be a continual thing.*
- *Let him know that you are there for him but that he has to make the change himself.*
- *No reminding him of his no-good father and his resemblance to him.*
- *Let him know that you have his back, and move forward.*

This is not the time to beat him down. He needs you to be there. We all make mistakes, or, in better words, *less than the best decisions* in some situations. I made a decision that was less than the best decision when I got pregnant, unwed, at the age of nineteen, but I did not allow that to hinder my goals in life. I had to readjust for that time in my life. I decided that my son was more important than running the streets and having a man snuggled up close to me who didn't mean me or my son any good. I wanted the best for my son, so I invested my time, energy, and love in him. Ladies, anything worth having is worth the struggle, and your son's future is well worth it.

If there is a felony involved, the situation gets a little harder for our boys and men, but it's not the end of the world or their lives. If your son is serious about turning his life around, then he will be able to overcome this hurdle in life; if he's not serious about it, then he will hold up that shield of excuses as a way of feeling sorry for himself. Don't allow him to get mad at the system because he landed in jail or has a record. Remember, it was his decision that got him where he is. The system just followed up by handing him a harder deck of cards with which to play the game of life. But life's cards aren't fair anyway, so tell him to suck it up and stick out his chest, because this is where you separate *the boys from the men*!

It's all about leaving boyhood behind and stepping into manhood at any and all costs. It requires work on part of the men. *Boys make excuses for their problems; men handle their problems.*

I did some research on getting jobs, housing, and aid for men who have a felony on their record. I can tell you that it's a rough journey, but it's still very doable! It was tough even for me to just research the information, and I don't have a record. I couldn't believe how nasty people could be to you when you are seeking services to assist individuals who are down-and-out! I can see how someone could get discouraged, but remember that God is still on the throne, and He will make a way for you even when the path is crooked! He is in complete control and will make your enemy your footstool. I had to remember that while I dealt with the attitudes at the different agencies and while the workers rolled their eyes because I was getting on their nerves by asking them to answer the questions that they were getting paid to answer.

Don't let that stop you! Remember what you are trying to accomplish. Keep your mind on your goal! We all encounter roadblocks in life, and believe me, you will have several on this journey. Don't take the roadblocks personally, but do take your journey personally. As the young people say, "Go on and brush your shoulders off," and keep moving!

Tips for Finding a Job

Men, go to your local unemployment office and explain to them that you are seeking employment but you have a felony on your record. They will have certain jobs that you can go out and interview for. They have those particular jobs coded in the system differently than others. Keep in mind that your choices maybe limited, but there are jobs out there to be found. I've held down three jobs at one time, so I know you can find work!

Look for jobs that do not require a background check (if you're applying on your own). Here are some suggestions:

- Construction work
- Delivering newspapers
- Truck driving
- Landscaping
- Janitorial work (with corporations)
- Grocery store clerk

- The fast-food industry
- Car mechanic
- Start your own towing company.
- Work for a temp agency.
- Learn a trade or create your own business.

No, these jobs are not glamorous, but the reason why you are in the position you are in now isn't glamorous either! Why live life in constant fear that you may end up behind bars, in jail, or dead because you refuse to live life by the rules? If you truly want to turn your life around, then you can. There are jobs out there. They may not be your dream jobs, but they pay a salary and allow you to be productive in society.

Proverbs 10:22 (KJV)
The blessing of the Lord, it maketh rich, and he addeth no sorrow with it.

Tips for Finding Housing

Believe it or not, being a felon even hinders your ability to secure someplace to live. I found out that in my area, if you have a felony that is less than five years old, most places will not allow you to rent an apartment. Depending on what the felony is for, you may not be allowed to rent an apartment even if your offense was more than five years ago.

Every bed is made according to how you put it together! If you made a "hard" bed, then you will have restless and sleepless nights or hard times; if your bed was made "soft," then nine times out of ten things will fall into place. Don't get mad at society because you made the decision you did—get mad at yourself and start moving towards a better tomorrow. Let go of the past and let God handle it! Nothing covered up can ever be seen! Deal with all situations, or they will deal with you!

Go to your local health department and ask about the different programs that they have for males in particular or anyone in need of assistance. I was surprised to find that men can get food stamps, temporary insurance, and assistance with housing. Remember, this is a temporary stepping-stone to help you get on your feet until you are able to do better. Do not get hooked into the system. Assistance programs are not made for long-term situations. A man without a plan ends up nowhere. You have a destination, and this is merely a pit stop on that journey!

Life has many bumps, turns, and bruises, but you must roll with every punch in order to grab onto your future. There are many routes to take. Some are shortcuts and then there's the long way around, but whatever path to achievement you take depends on you. If you are on the long path because of a bump in the road that landed you on the wrong side of the law, remember that you still have a future to walk toward, so keep moving forward with this information in one hand and your plan for your life in the other.

Home is where the heart is. Home is where our boys draw their strength and their security in life. Home should be a safe place and a soft place to fall. Ladies, as children, our young boys see and experience life through our life decisions and experiences. So we must build a solid foundation for the home in which to properly raise our young boys.

Proverbs 4:20–27 (NLT)
Pay attention, my child, to what I say. Listen carefully. Don't lose sight of my words. Let them penetrate deep within your heart, for they bring life and radiant health to anyone who discovers their meaning. Above all else, guard your heart, for it affects everything you do. Avoid all perverse talk; stay far from corrupt speech. Look straight ahead, and fix your eyes on what lies before you. Mark out a straight path for your feet; then stick to the path and stay safe. Don't get sidetracked; keep your feet from following evil.

CHAPTER 13

MOTIVATION

Proverbs 14:1 (NLT)
A wise woman builds her house; a foolish woman tears hers down with her own hands.

Ladies, we must make sure that we build our children up from the inside out and not the outside in. We must fill them with love, hope, self-esteem, will, drive, compassion, and healthy living, but we can't do that if we don't have those very things inside of us. So what we must do is build a healthier you. In this section of the book we are going to do just that by giving you the proper tools that are necessary. I am going to share with you some small tips that can and will help you if you take the time to apply them in your life. I know change is not easy and that new things are a challenge, but we can only move as far as we are willing to walk. It's your life and your journey. How far are you willing to walk to better your quality of living? Martin Luther King Jr. walked miles for you, and he didn't even know you personally. But he loved you enough to walk endless, tiresome miles just for you, and you know that Jesus died and gave his life for you. Look at how precious and special you are that Jesus was born and died in order for you to have life and have it more abundantly. Don't let him down. Think about that cross he had to bear, and then your cross in life won't seem as hard. Stand up and be responsible and accountable for your life.

Proverbs 21:25 (NLT)
The desires of lazy people will be their ruin, for their hands refuse to work.

OK, first thing that I want to share with you is on your inner beauty. Your personal spirit is the key to your success in life. Some may call your inner beauty your personality, but I like to call it your personal spirit.

You must begin by loving who you are on the inside. God made you special. He gave each and every one of us a special something about us. Everyone is made to be the designer's original; no two people are exactly the same. Even identical twins have something different about them. What's your special feature, the thing that you have the rights to, the patent to that no one else can duplicate? It could be your golden smile, the way that you articulate your words, or the way that you walk with your head lifted up to the sky. It also could be the way that you love. It is whatever you feel is special and unique about you and your soul.

If you don't know who you are or what makes you unique, then you need to sit back and search your innermost feelings and thoughts. One thing is true and should be foremost in your thoughts: God didn't make a mistake with you. You are his very best, poured into that vessel called your body, and it's a temple not to be tainted or tampered with.

I used to think that God made a mistake by not allowing me to have hips and a big butt. My sister has a big butt with wide hips, and so do several of my girlfriends. I would think, *How can a sister be a sister without our signature in life—a butt!* I was looking at the physical and not my spiritual or inner beauty. I used to joke about buying myself a big butt and a pair of wide hips when I became rich, but now I tell everybody that God knew exactly what he was doing by not giving me hips and a big butt, because otherwise I wouldn't be the person I am today. Now that I have grown spiritually and strengthened my inner beauty, I know that my flesh, my body, means nothing without my inside being healthy and whole. I could have the body measurements of "36–24–36"—a "brick house," as we used to call it back in my day—and still be unhappy and unsatisfied with who I was as a person. Now I thank God for every inch of my body and the inner beauty it possesses. I love me, even with my big feet, big nose, short stature, and dark skin. Believe it or not, those things that I just mentioned are things I used to hate because people used to tease me all the time about them, but now they are my favorite features on my body. Life has a way of changing things the longer you live. Every day I thank God for life and love because my life is so precious and special to me. I still encounter problems in my life, but now I know how to ride out those waves differently. Some waves require only a surf board, another may require a canoe, and then there are others that require you to be in a boat with a life jacket strapped to your back—but through life experience I now know how to recognize what vessel is most useful when going through a tough situation.

I love the Serenity Prayer: "God, grant me the serenity to accept the things I cannot change, courage to change the things I can, and wisdom to know the difference." Those words make good sense for easy living. Why worry? I try to count everything that happens in my life—good or bad—as joy and turn it over to the Lord. In other words, change what you can; what you can't change turn over to the Lord, and don't worry about things we can't change. For example, when we are sick to our stomachs and need to vomit, we tend to resist the natural thing to do. We try our hardest not to bring up the impurities that our body is naturally trying to expel, which would allow us to feel better. I don't know if we try to hold onto situations because we are scared that someone may see the mess we've made and may judge us; or if it's because we don't like the way it feels when we are directly confronted; or if we feel that we have no control over the situation.

The truth of the matter is the more we try to hold onto things, the bigger the explosion afterwards. The mess you were trying to cover up and keep hidden makes a bigger mess upon its exit, leaving you sitting and wondering why you held onto that mess for so long. When things come about and you feel that you have no way out, let go and let God. He will allow you to try to fix your situation, but he'll also let you see that you should have left well enough alone and depended on Him.

Ladies, let's truly, truly start loving who we are, because the fact of the matter is no matter what you try to change on the outside, if you don't feel good on the inside you are still a "dead girl walking!" Plus, wherever you go you are still there, so you might as well accept the real you!

I want to share some things with you to help place you on the right track to feeling good about yourself, which will in turn allow you to feel good when interacting with others. The two most important things in helping you achieve a healthier you are your thinking and your speech. Life is in the power of the tongue. You speak life or death into your life and over your situations. What you think about is what you gravitate towards. It's true: what you expect out of life is what you get. I expect the abundant life and nothing but God's very best for me in my health, spirituality, physical being, finances, social settings, family, and friends.

Helpful Nuggets

- *Know and believe that God loves you and that he died for you.*
- *Believe that you are special and unique.*
- *Find out what you are passionate about.*
- *Drop any and all dead weights; they only weigh you down.*

Ladies, let's get things started by getting our personal lives in order. A house that has order knows where it stands! Our finances play a very important role in our lives. Our finances determine where we live, how we are able to provide for our families, and our future existence. The next half of the book is dedicated to you and your future. I dedicated the first half of the book to rearing and encouraging our young men, but now it's all about you and your footing in life. I would like to walk through this with you together.

CHAPTER 14

FINANCE

Proverbs 13:7 (NLT)
Some who are poor pretend to be rich; others who are rich pretend to be poor.

Your finance is very important. It's the center of your life's existence. Your income determines so much of your life, so don't take it lightly.

Who are you? Are you the rich man, the poor man, the beggar man, or the thief? Are you robbing Peter to pay Paul? If so, then you are the thief. Ladies, are you robbing yourself and your future of the brightness you deserve? If you are living above your means, you need to stop, drop, and roll. Your finances are on fire and need to be extinguished right now before the whole house burns down. You need to get a handle on reality and put yourself in check. If you don't, you will never be able to see your way clear. I propose that you sit down and find out your true financial situation, and be very honest about it. Fooling yourself isn't going to help your situation at all—that's like putting a bandage on a broken arm and expecting it to heal in a couple of days. Your bandage isn't going to make your arm heal or make the pain go away, so let's get down to handling our business. It's time to uncover and expose that thief spirit.

There are three obstacles keeping you from financial freedom, and *numero uno* is false affluence—keeping up with the Joneses—pretending to be what you are not by overspending and trying to look wealthy. Image is everything to some people—sometimes it even means the death of the one who is trying to keep up the image. The *second* thing is lack of control. You need to be able to control your spending without thinking that you are depriving yourself. The *third* is commitment. You need to stay committed to a better quality of life by getting your finances under control. Ladies, I know you can do it. I am here for you: if you take one step, I am willing to take the second step with you. I am putting my steps in writing for you because you are worth the time and effort of placing your life on the right path to improving your finances.

The First Steps to Financial Freedom

List all your sources of income. Only include true income, such as your full-time job, a steady second job, child support, alimony, monthly bonuses, etc.

Keep a record to help determine where your money is going. Make a list of where your money is being spent and how much is being spent. Tracking it for a week or two will allow you to see if you are spending wisely or not.

Identify problem areas and take steps to resolve them. Once you have determined a problem area, you should red flag it. You need to find out if it is a need or a want. You may have to readjust your needs, but your wants need to be reduced to the bare minimum.

Develop a record-keeping system. You really need to keep good records for two very important reasons. One is that you need to always know who you owe and how much you owe. The second is that doing so allows you to know exactly where you stand … or where you are sitting, in some cases.

Check your payroll exemptions to make sure you are withholding the proper amount. There is nothing worse than finding out that you owe the government taxes and still don't have enough money to pay your bills. You don't want to cheat yourself, either, so make sure you are taking out the right amount of withholdings to get the most on your payroll check.

Evaluate your company benefits. Take a close look at the benefits that are offered by your employer, such as your 401(k), retirement benefits, and life, health, and disability insurance. Take advantage of your 401(k); most company these day match your dollars up to a certain percent after you have worked a specific amount of years for the company and have become vested. If you are tight on money, only deduct up to the amount that your employer begins to match your deduction. Check to see if your company pays for benefits that you are not aware of. Some companies pay the entire medical benefit if it's only employee coverage and may contribute a certain percentage towards family coverage.

Who Are You?

Are you always whining and crying about being broke? Do you never have enough money, and are you always looking for a handout? Then you are the "beggar man," always needing to be rescued. You have so many life jackets on that you are beginning to sink. Your rescuers originally gave you their life jackets to help keep you from drowning, but the weight from all of the different accumulated jackets is beginning to take you under. What was meant to help you is now a hindrance because you have not learned how to balance and maintain your finances on your own, so you continue to sink further and further into debt. I am willing to take another step with you to help get you through the next step that you must take in order to move forward in this process and remove some of those life jackets.

Proverbs 10:15-16 (NLT)
The wealth of the rich is their fortress; the poverty of the poor is their calamity. The earnings of the godly enhance their lives, but evil people squander their money on sin.

You must decide where you want to go from here.

Set realistic goals, both long- and short-term. This is serious business. I need you to seriously act on setting your goals; if you don't have a clear vision of your goals, then how can you possibly know where you are going and whether you have arrived? Start with a short-term goal, such as paying off the smallest bill that you have. You can even set very simple goals, such as saving five dollars a week and not touching it, no matter what. Whatever the goal is, write it down and scratch it off once you have obtained it. You will feel so much better when you can actually see what you are accomplishing. Remember, small steps turn into big ones. Long-term goals take much more time, dedication, and will power because it takes longer to see the results of your hard work. Your long-term goals can be things such as buying a house within five years, paying off your larger debt by a set time, starting a business, retirement, or just plain old being debt-free and sitting under a cool shade tree before your fortieth birthday.

Prioritize your goals. Work on what's most important to you first. We tend to entertain the things that are important to us in life. Remember, where you see smoke there is guaranteed to be a fire, and we are trying to put out all fires that can possibly burn down our house.

Review and revise your goals periodically. Once you start working on your set goals, you may find a better way to approach them than you originally thought. You also might find that what you thought was important before isn't so important now.

Are You?

The poor man and the beggar man are cohabiting buddies. It's time to actually take off one of those life preservers to save you. You will find that it feels good to be able to float on your own, even if you have to lie on your back, floating face up in the hot, scorching sun. You can do it. I have faith in you.

The last man standing is the rich man. If you fall into this category, all I can say to you is to keep on doing what you are doing. Keep formulating your plans and continue to do what I outline in this chapter. Don't forget that I am here with you, stepping in the name of love and putting it in writing so you can step on, too.

Revise your spending. Continue to cut out unnecessary possessions, such as extra cars that are not being used. They come with added expenses—insurance, maintenance, tags, etc. Get rid of expensive gadgets and pieces of equipment. Do you really need that new cell phone just because it has the capability of taking pictures, or that iPod because it's the "in" thing?

Become an informed consumer. Shop wisely.

Plan your credit use. Please do not use your credit as an extension of your income. Doing that is living off of borrowed money that you don't really have and paying for its use twice and sometimes three times, depending on your interest rates. But you already know this because you are the rich man. Most rich people are not the ones riding around in expensive vehicle throwing money out of the window but are the ones who are making wise decisions about their spending habits and savings.

Limit your total debt. Do not spend over 20 percent of your net monthly income (take-home pay) on incoming debt or spending. Your rent or mortgage should be no higher than 28 percent of your net income (take-home pay).

Pay bills. You need to develop a system for paying your bills. What we make a habit of doing over and over becomes automatic.

Save for rainy days and snowstorms. You need to start putting away for the stormy days that are unexpected, such as a car breaking down, the roof leaking, one of the kids needing dental work, and other emergencies that are not part of your day-to-day survival. Storms come and go, but you want to be prepared for them by having the right storm gear to protect you. Why stand out in a rainstorm with mittens on and a snow shovel in your hand, or stand in a snowstorm with rain boots on and an umbrella? You need to be prepared with the right equipment for the storms that you will experience in life. View your financial planning as an ongoing process.

Let's take a quick recap of the main things we need to keep in mind:

- Set realistic goals and expectations.
- Develop a true plan that you can live with.
- Adjust your plan as your goals are reached and/or family circumstances and income change.
- Take control of the money that you have by becoming financially free, rather than letting your money having control of you.

Proverbs 12:24 (NLT)
Work hard and become a leader; be lazy and become a slave.

Nuggets of Information to Help Reduce Your Monthly Expenses

Clothing:
Buy clothing that's machine washable and doesn't require dry cleaning.
Hang clothes on a clothesline to dry instead of using a dryer.
Have children change into old clothes to play in.

Do not buy clothes that require dry-cleaning.

Organize laundry so that a minimum number of loads are run each week.

Sew clothing for you and your family as much as you can and repair damaged articles, when possible, instead of discarding them.

Carefully coordinate what you buy, to allow more use for each item.

Medical:

Serve nutritious meals.

Have regular checkups.

Carry only health and accident insurance.

Find out what services are offered by the local health department.

Use immunization clinics.

Learn to take temperature, pulse, and respiration rates.

Learn about symptoms of common diseases in order to determine if seeing a doctor is necessary.

Develop good health habits.

Stop using tobacco, alcohol, and any other addictive drugs.

Child-care:

Share child-care responsibilities with a good friend or neighbor.

Check out facilities that are operated for low-income families (for example, government- or church-operated nursery schools).

Gifts and donations:

Make gifts instead of buying them.

Give your time instead of your money.

Carefully consider each situation and cut out all monetary giving that you possibly can.

Pay close attention to the following sections. These are areas in which we throw away the most money, but believe it or not, these are the areas in which we can save the most.

Food:

Cook only as much as can be eaten.

Take your lunch to work.

Buy in quantity if it's cheaper.

Limit junk food purchases.

Use leftovers in soups and casseroles.

Plan meals in advance and stick to the plan.

Use coupons for items that you regularly buy.

Make a grocery list and stick to it.

Recreation and entertainment:
Consider the cost of habits such as smoking.
Attend high school sports events.
Have potluck dinners at home instead of going out to eat.
Take vacations close to home to save on lodging and gas.
Cancel your cable TV service.
Use public parks and picnic areas.
Rent movies instead of going out to see movies in theaters.

Transportation:
Buy used vehicles.
Use public transportation.
If you have more than one car, get rid of one.
Consider moving closer to work.
Drive small cars that cost less to operate.
Eliminate unnecessary car trips.
Do your own vehicle maintenance.
Carpool.

Household:
Use glass instead of paper cups.
Learn how to do simple home repairs.
Mow your own lawn.
Do your own decorating and painting.
Use lights only when necessary.
Adjust your thermostat at night; lower it in cold weather and raise it in hot weather.
Remove all of the bells and whistles from your phone service.
Conserve water.
Take advantage of public utility programs to lower electricity and water costs.

In addition, remember the importance of savings ...

Savings:
Try to save regularly.
Use savings only for true emergencies.
Automatically deduct savings from your paycheck each pay period.

Proverbs 10:14a (NLT)
Wise people treasure knowledge.

CHAPTER 15

KEYS TO SUCCESSFUL BUDGETING

No one like to budget, but a budget is beneficial you and your family.

Make sure your information is accurate. Make sure that you are working with the most current information possible concerning the bills you are paying each month and the income that you have coming in. You do not want to over- or underestimate either of the two. The more accurate your information, the better chance you have of being able to set a true budget.

Make sure you count your regular (monthly, quarterly, etc.) bills. Sit down and make up a list of every single thing that you make payments on, even the bills that you may pay every three or six months.

To get the monthly payment amounts for the bills you pay quarterly or semiyearly, all you have to do is divide the total payment by the number of months. For example, if you pay $600 every three months, you would divide $600 by three to get $200 a month. You need to add the $200 to your monthly budget so that when it comes due you won't be surprised and have to scramble around to come up with the payment.

Track everything you buy for a couple of months. The best way to stay on top of your budget until you get a handle on budgeting is to track your spending. This will allow you to see where your money is going and if you are spending your money unwisely. In other words, are you wishing upon a star by buying thirty dollars' worth of lottery tickets every week when your dreams can come true by saving a dollar or two per week?

Tracking your spending is the easiest way for you to identify your weak areas of unnecessary spending. We all have areas in which we could spend less, and I am guilty, too. I love buying any kind of journal because I love to write. I really had to pace myself when it came to buying cute journals with cute little phrases or inspirational quotes on the cover. I found myself rationalizing my unnecessary spending by telling myself, "It only costs a dollar," but those single dollars add up to several dollars. What I started doing in my mind was "handcuffing" myself because I was committing the worst crime against myself—I was robbing my future. I was guilty of spending unnecessarily. Every time those imaginary "cuffs" were placed on my wrists, I became mindful of my spending. When I felt like buying a cute journal because it was a dollar, I saw my hands cuffed together, and I knew that I had to refrain from buying that item. In my mind I no longer had the freedom to move my hands in the direction of picking up that item to carry it to the register. If you are guilty of unnecessary spending, then you need to be cuffed, too!

Buy things that you really need, not things that you want. We all have the habit of wanting to satisfy our desires. Sometimes all we can think is, *I want that dress! Forget about how expensive it is and the bills I owe—I want that dress!* The same dress that you couldn't live without will have you sleepless in Seattle and worried about a bill you could have paid instead. Try buying only the things that are necessary and not what you desire because "you just have to have it."

Make a shopping list. I believe in shopping lists; they really work, as long as you stick to the list. We all know or have an idea of how much our usual purchases cost. By writing your list and estimating a budget that you must stick to, you will eliminate unnecessary spending. Only go down the aisles that contain the items on your shopping list, so you won't be tempted to buy extra things. Don't forget to add your BOGO's to your list, your buy one and get one free, but don't allow the getting the second item free have you over thinking the necessity of buying when you know you will never need it. I'm guilty of over stocking with BOGO's to the point that some items had gone to waste. We don't want wasteful spending, but instead smart shopping!

Shop on a full stomach. I believe in the saying, "Don't grocery shop on an empty stomach, or you will buy more than you intended." I know for a fact that I tend to buy more when I am hungry than when I'm full. Now, that could be all in my mind, but when I'm shopping on an empty stomach I find myself picking up little things that I normally wouldn't purchase, and that's a waste of my hard-earned cash! That's called wasteful spending, Remember, we are trying to save and not spend!

Use coupons or take advantage of sales. Using store coupons can save the day and some money, too! There are some women who cut out every single coupon in the paper and use them because the items are on sale. I suggest that you cut out coupons just for items that you normally purchase. After all, time is money, and you are trying to save money! Plus, are you really saving if you are buying things that you don't need just because they are on sale? In addition, shop on weekdays when the stores are running their sales instead of on the weekend, when the sales are coming to an end and most sale items have already been purchased.

Don't shop every other day. If you are running to the store every other day, picking up items here and there, stop it! Stop it right now! You are pouring your money down the drain. You spend more money by purchasing items here and there, in part because you tend to grab items that you don't even need. Treat stores like they have the plague, and stay far away from them unless you have to grocery shop. Even if you are shopping for clothing, stay away from the malls. We tend to spend more by window-shopping. Take control of your money; don't let your money take control of you!

Buy in bulk if possible. You can save greatly by shopping at the superstores or store clubs, like Sam's Club and Costco. Some things are better purchased in bulk, for example, dishwashing detergent, laundry detergent, bath soap, and toilet paper—things that are used on a daily base or have high rates of consumption. Buying nonperishable food in bulk is good idea if you have a large family. Of course, there's no sense in buying food in bulk if it perishes before you get a chance to use it.

Take your lunch to work. You must take your lunch! The bottom line is it saves you money. It's OK to go out to lunch with your coworkers sometimes, but going out daily can dig deep into your pockets unnecessarily. Here is the deal: most lunches cost anywhere from five to ten dollars, depending on where you are eating. Spending five dollars every weekday adds up to one hundred dollars a month, and if your lunch costs ten dollars daily, that's two hundred dollars a month! I'm no mathematician, but that's a lot of money that you could have saved or put towards paying down your debt. Stop pointing the gun at your foot. Aren't you tired of wounding yourself? Even though these kinds of wounds are sometimes superficial and may heal easily, why go through the unnecessary pain? Take the time to plan your lunch and start packing each day—your lunch, that is!

Look for sales or off-season bargains. I used to laugh at my mother because she would come home bragging about what she had saved by shopping at the after-Christmas sales—but the joke was on me, because it's a great way to save. I remember my mother buying an eight-dollar box of Christmas cards for one dollar, wrapping paper for seventy-five cents, tape for twenty-five cents, and Christmas ornaments for close to nothing. I thought she was crazy! I later found out that she was a smart shopper! You can really get great bargains—especially on clothing—by shopping off-season. Believe it or not, the clothes are not out of style and are just as hip as the clothes on the shelf that season.

I used to shop for my son at JC Penney on Wednesdays, because they always put out their sale items on that day. I had to make my way to the back of the store to the men's department to find the three racks of clothing that were on sale, but the savings were worth the hunt! I saved greatly! The downside to off-season shopping is the limit of choice. Always try to compare price. When you shop smart, you win in the end! Compare prices!

Buy a used car instead of a new car. You may not have the "new-car smell" that we all want when we purchase a car, but you will save thousands of dollars by purchasing a used car—and that smell is sweeter than any new-car smell any day!

Do you know that the moment you drive off the lot with your new car it depreciates in value? Your monthly payments can be hundreds of dollars more a month for a new car versus a used car. You don't have to purchase a car that is four or five years old. You can buy a year-old car that has never been owned before and still save yourself some green! Guess what? They have the new-car smell! Buy used!

I made the mistake of buying new, and I paid for it (literally) every time I had to write out a check to make those payments. I began to feel like I had a life sentence hanging over my head … but I had that new car! I can tell you that was the longest five years ever! And because of my decision to buy a new car with higher payments, I had to become a thief: I ended up having to rob Peter to pay Paul to make good on my car payments! Juggling money around that should have been used to pay another bill.

Having a new car even with higher payments feels great until the excitement wears off around the sixth month. Then the honeymoon is over, and the new-car smell is gone, too! But guess what? Yes, those payments are still hanging around staring you in the face! Just be careful and don't get hooked!

Discontinue services you don't need, such as cable, cell phones, or pagers. If you don't need these gadgets, then let go of them! They are draining the life out of you and your bank account! Don't pay for convenience when convenience is inconveniencing you! Those services add up monthly!

Avoid rent-to-own centers and check-cashing stores. All I have to say is: I am guilty! I rented furniture through a rent-to-own center until I found out that they had all but pierced my jugular vein and I was practically bleeding to death. I thank God that a light clicked on for me. I paid almost triple for my furniture, but had I just waited until I had the money to make a wise purchase or had found a store that would allow me to place my furniture on layaway, I would have saved myself some money! I was paying fifty dollars a week for a stereo that cost no more than three hundred dollars in a regular store, all because of the desire to have the stereo right then and there! At that time I didn't do the math because I wanted that stereo! But it would have taken me eighteen months to pay it off! The best way to stay out of this trap is to stay out of their trap! I'm sorry¾I meant their stores!

I am guilty again! Baby, let me tell you that those check-cashing centers will have you hooked like a fish trying to wiggle your way off of their line! I remember being in a rut and needing five hundred dollars. I had nowhere else to turn, so I turned to a convenient payday loan center. They were so nice and polite. They allowed me to write them a check, and they were even gracious enough to hold my check for me for a month without cashing it. But little did I know that I was still going to be five hundred dollars in the hole when the next month came around. What do you think I had to do again? Right! Get another loan from them to pay for the previous loan. I found myself on this crazy merry-go-round for months until I got tired of going around and around and around! I finally was able to take the hit of the paying back my loan without taking out a new loan. Please try at all cost to avoid these places—remember, we pay out the "backside" for convenience.

Use cash, not credit. It's better to use cash than credit; you tend to think twice if you are spending your own money. If you must purchase something on credit, make sure you set a spending limit and stick to it. Remember, you will pay three to five times more for that item if you pay by credit and if you pay only the minimum each month.

If you must use a credit card, try to pay the balance off each month; at the very least, you will be saving on the interest. It might take years to pay off your balance, depending on your balance owed.

Spending on credit is like jumping into a black hole, and once you fall into its trap it will swallow you up. You will continue to free-fall until you somehow get a handle on things before hitting rock bottom. More about credit is discussed in the next chapter.

Steps to making a budget:
- List your net income.
- List your monthly expenses.
- Set aside an emergency reserve.
- Compare income to expenses.
- Set priorities (goals) and make changes so that your income will be greater than your expenses.

Helpful nuggets to increase your income:
- Work overtime hours.
- Find a part-time job.
- Sell goods that you make at home.
- Sell items that you no longer need; have a garage sale or take them to a flea market.

I know that this must seem like a lot to take in and a lot of hard work, but nothing good in life ever comes easy.

Proverbs 12:11 (NLT) Hard work means prosperity; only fools idle away their time.

CHAPTER 16

CREDIT

Your credit touches every aspect of your life, including your chances of employment.

This section of the book is dedicated with our young men in mind and also to help you get things on track to building and creating a solid foundation called a home for him, after all home is where the heart is! And his heart and soul is what we are trying to encourage! A hefty dose of self esteem and stability will take you a long way, so I encourage you to free your mind and open your heart and start stacking one brick at a time to help build that solid foundation called stability. Most people when they are on stable grounds feel good about themselves, so Ladies when you feel good about whom you are then you are able to share that confidence with someone else like our young boys!

What is credit? Credit could be a ray of sunshine or a dark cloud hovering over your head, depending on your credit score. Credit means you are using someone else's money to pay for things that you can't really afford in cash. You make a promise to repay the money to the person or company that loaned you the money. A loan usually includes both principal (money that you borrowed) and interest (the additional money you pay for borrowing their money). Good credit simply means that you make your loan payments on time and as promised. If you repay your debt on time, you will experience the "sunshine" side of credit; but if you just pay whenever it's convenient for you, then you better be ready for those dark storm clouds to roll in.

Collection agencies are like bloodhounds—they can sniff you out from under a rock even if you're in the deep jungles of Africa hiding. They will come up beside you on a big, gray elephant talking about how your bill is delinquent and you need to make an arrangement to get it paid! Seriously, not paying your obligations back causes the heat to turn up in your life, and more heat equals more stress, and stress is a silent killer. We are trying to bring forth life, not take it away!

Sometimes we think that credit is free money, that "they" can't make you pay it back, and so what if it goes on your credit record? How many times have we used the adage "you can't get blood from a turnip"? It's true, but that ulcer in the pit of your stomach from worrying will cause bleeding internally. Good credit is very important and necessary in this world, so we need to find a way to get a handle on this situation. You need credit if you plan on purchasing large items such as a house or a car. Yes, you can still purchase those items with dings on your credit, but you will pay a higher interest rate, and in the long run that means more money out of your pocket. Nowadays, everything you do revolve around your credit score. If you apply for a job, most places check your credit history. Companies feel that your credit history gives them an overview or snapshot of who you are; it shows if you are a responsible person. Most major insurance companies are checking your credit score before making a decision about whether they want to insure you. If you have low scores, you may pay higher premiums and larger down payments, and some companies may even turn you down. The major systems that drive the world now are credit-driven. We must get it together if we want the best for our families; we must set good examples for them. You need to find out as much as you can about credit—the good side and the bad side—so you can pass that information on to our young boys. First thing first, you need to find out what your credit score is. I suggest that you request a copy of your credit report from one of the three credit reporting agencies or Credit Karma:

Equifax
1-800- 685-1111
www.equifax.com

Experian
1-888-EXPERIAN (397-3742)
www.experian.com

Trans Union
1-800-916-8800
www.transunion.com

Credit Karma
www.creditkarma.com

You can request an individual copy of your credit report from each company, or you can merge the results of all three agencies at one time. You can also request a copy of your report from only one company to see how you are being rated by them, but keep in mind that your score from one agency may not be the same as the scores from the other agencies because some companies (creditors) may only report to one of the three agencies. I suggest that you pull all three reports, especially if you are trying to purchase a home. Normally, when purchasing a home, the mortgage lenders request your credit history from all three agencies. Car loan companies may use one specific agency. You should order your credit report at least once a year. Some states may have a law that requires credit reporting agencies to provide you with one or two free reports every year; if not, there is normally a small fee per credit report. You can also request a free copy of your credit report if you were turned down for a loan.

Your credit score is based on your history of repaying your obligations or debts and is used to predict how likely you will repay a new loan. Generally, creditors/lenders look at the last one or two years of your bill-paying history to determine if you are a good candidate for a loan.

Credit scores are calculated based on how you make your payments each month. If you pay on time every month, then it's a positive point for you. Charging your credit cards to their limit is a negative point. The computer calculates the positive and the negative points, and the resulting number is your credit score.

What's considered a good credit score may vary from lender to lender, depending on their credit-scoring model. Scores may range from three hundreds to nine hundreds. Each lender decides what's considered to be a good credit risk or a poor credit risk for their individual company, so it's best for them to explain to you what your credit score mean in terms of their final credit decision about your credit worthiness. Normally, the better your score the better of your chance to get an approval.

Helpful nuggets on improving low or poor credit scores:
- Pay your bills on time every month.
- Charge less than the maximum amount available on your credit card.
- Try to pay more than the minimum due on your credit card each month.
- Only apply for credit that you need (such as for a mortgage).
- Look for ways to cut your expense and/or increase your income.
- Keep track of your bills and "past due" notices.
- Remember that credit cards are loans and not free money.

How can you obtain credit if you have no credit history?

There are nontraditional means of establishing a credit history:
- Ask any established companies to which you already make payments to write you a letter of reference. The letter can come from your landlord, the telephone company, the gas company, etc. Ask them to include how long you have been a customer and to discuss your ability or history of paying them each month.

- Keep copies of all bills you pay.
- Keep copies of the canceled checks or money orders used to pay your bills as your proof of payment.

You need to show at least two years of regular payment history, although some agencies may only require one year.

CHAPTER 17

BANKING

Banking is important and opening a checking and savings account is a must.

Some of us don't trust banks, but I am here to tell you that banking is a much safer way to handle your money. I was shocked to find that people are still hiding money under mattresses and in shoeboxes, pillowcases, socks, or far back in the corners of their closets. We really need to stop that right about now—and below are some great reasons why!

Placing your money in a bank can save you a lot of money, and there are other great benefits attached to banking with a bank or credit union. You receive interest on your money, and they offer you great deals if you finance your loans through them. Plus, if your money isn't at your fingertips, then it's not so readily available for you to spend it. You also save on fees that are associated with purchasing money orders and having a check-cashing center cash your check. Think about the convenience and all of the time it will save you from running all around town trying to buy a money order or looking for a check-cashing center to cash your check. Have your check direct-deposited to your account. Talk about convenience—direct deposit is the ultimate! Sometimes your money is in your account a day before you get paid! Now that's what I'm talking about!

Checking Accounts

Hear me out when I say you really must keep a handle on your checking account by making sure that it stays balanced. You don't want any rubber checks to bounce, nor does your bank. Here are some reasons why: First of all, it's a felony to write worthless checks. Secondly, depending on the amount, you could face jail time. And third—but least of all—you will acquire return fees that you must pay to your banking institution and to the parties to whom you wrote the bad checks. If you don't have a checking account, let's get busy on making that happen!

Savings Accounts

Savings accounts are just as important as checking accounts. A dollar a day will help keep the rain away! A saving account could help you get through a rainy day, but do not nickel and dime your way out of your savings. The easiest way to improve your overall monthly financial picture is through savings.

Credit Unions vs. Banks

Shopping around is the best way to find out whether a credit union or a bank is better for you. There are several things that you need to find out, such as whether there is a minimum balance requirement and if there's a charge if you drop below that balance. Also, find out the amount of interest you will receive on your money for placing your money with their institution. Credit unions normally give their members better perks than banks do, but, as always, you need to find the right institution that fits your needs.

The FDIC (bank)/NCUA (credit union) ensure that your money will be safe and available to you, so make sure you look for their posted signs in financial institutions, or inquire about it. There is a limit to how much the FDIC/NCUA will insure your money, so be sure to verify that limit.

CHAPTER 18

BUYING A HOME

Buying home has so many benefits and establishing wealth is one of the benefits.

Buying a home is part of the American dream. Dorothy said it best in *The Wizard of Oz*: "There's no place like home!" So, here we are in my favorite part of the book—real estate! Now that we have our act together and our affairs in check, it's time to move forward. This will probably be one of the most important and scariest decision-making processes that you will ever have to go through, but I am here to make it a little bit easier for you. For the record, I am a licensed real-estate agent in the state of Florida, and I believe in the American dream of owning your own home.

Ladies, I want to start off by saying, "I believe in you, and you can do all things through Christ Jesus, who strengthens you!" And because I believe in you, this time I am going to take the first step and allow you to follow by taking the second step. See, you are not alone. I am going to give you some valuable tips that will help make your home-buying process less stressful! This process can be overwhelming if you let it, but remember: "I can do all things through Christ Jesus, who strengthens me!" Our Father didn't bring you this far to leave you, just as He has your back I got it, too! All of the support and help you need is right here for you. Oh, one more thing while I am thinking about it: never buy a home if you will outgrow it in a year or two, or if you are planning to relocate in a couple of years—it's just wasted money.

Proverbs 13:9a (NLT)
The life of the godly is full of light and joy.

Helpful Nuggets for Buying a Home

Step one: Get pre-qualified for a mortgage.

The very first thing you must do before contacting a realtor is get pre-qualified for a loan to buy a home. This process is so important, and it should be your number one priority in looking for the perfect home. Getting pre-qualified in advance helps your realtor to find the right house for you based on what you can comfortably afford. The process is simple, all you have to do is provide your income and your debt obligation to your loan officer and they will pull your credit and then provide you with a letter stating what you may be approved for based on your credit score and income.

You wouldn't believe how many people actually start this process backwards by first finding a realtor to help them find a house, only to find out later that the loan they thought they qualified for was much less than what they had expected or they didn't qualify at all. Their hard work and effort—and the effort of their realtor—were in vain. The flip side is you may actually qualify for a bigger loan than you expected so, start off by getting pre-qualified first to avoid any undue stress.

There are several ways to obtain a home loan, such as going through your local bank or credit union, a mortgage broker, private lending, or by a referral, etc. There are several types of loans and programs available to you. I suggest that you take your time and shop around for the best mortgage and program for you and your financial situation. I am very serious when I say that you really need to shop around, because the wrong loan will have you "stuck like chuck!" There is nothing worse than moving into a new home and feeling like you are trapped in a prison. Make sure that you understand the ins and outs of the loan, the different fees charged, and the terms of the loan. Make sure that the loan officer goes over the penalties as well.

Call several companies to get information about their programs, but do not allow all of them to pull your credit. Only allow the one that you are seriously considering to pull your credit, because every time your credit is pulled, it shows on your record, and that affects your rating.

Check your local newspaper—it's a great way to get a good idea of the current interest rates. Rates are normally listed in the real-estate section of your local paper.

Step two: Obtain a mortgage.

There are several options available to you when trying to obtain a mortgage loan. You really need to have an idea of what type of loan best fits you. You should ask yourself: are you looking for a loan that only requires you to come up with

5 percent down and has a fixed rate? Are you going to need assistance with your down payment? Or are you looking to put nothing down at all? These are just a few questions you should ask yourself before you seek a mortgage loan. There are so many programs available, so you really need to compare and "shop 'til you drop." I know you know how to "shop 'til you drop," so pretend that you're at your favorite store and they are having a blue light special!

Ladies, if you decide to go with an adjustable rate mortgage (ARM), know that the rates on these loans adjust at a certain time. If you are not careful and have not planned accordingly, once the rate adjusts to the current rate you will be in a pickle and won't be able to pay your mortgage. You might go into foreclosure. ARMs aren't altogether a bad idea, though. They allow you another avenue to get into a home when you have less than perfect credit. But if you can avoid an ARM, then I suggest you do so!

If your loan officer has to elaborately finagle a way for you to get into your home, then you really can't afford the home. Not everybody who has been placed in an ARM loan program is in that position, but a lot of people are. I believe that if you have to play around in order to get into the home, then it's not worth it. You will be sorry and unable to enjoy your home. Personally, I don't care for an ARM mortgage, but some people swear by them, so if you decide to go that route, please make sure you plan for the time when your rates will adjust. I would hate to see you stuck and looking crazy because you didn't have the funds to pay your new mortgage payment!

Fixed rate mortgage—The interest rate doesn't change the entire term of the mortgage loan.

Adjustable rate mortgage (ARM)—A mortgage that allows the lender to adjust its interest rate periodically on the basis of changes in the specific index.

Conventional mortgage—Any mortgage that isn't insured or guaranteed by the Federal Housing Administration.

FHA mortgage—A mortgage insured by the Federal Housing Administration.

VA loan—Guaranteed by the U.S. Department of Veterans Affairs.

Lease purchase mortgage loan—A mortgage product that allows a homebuyer to lease a home from a nonprofit with an option to buy (renting to own). The monthly rent consists of PITI (principle, interest, taxes, and insurance) payments on the first mortgage, plus an extra amount that is deposited into a savings account and that eventually becomes your down payment.

3/2 option—This product allows low- and moderate-income borrowers to put only 3 percent down of their own funds, coupled with a 2 percent gift from a relative, or a 2 percent grant, or a loan from a nonprofit, state, or local government agency. This particular mortgage product is offered through Fannie Mae.

First mortgage—A mortgage that has first claim to the secured property in the event that you should default on the loan.

Second mortgage—A mortgage that is second place to your first mortgage.

Notice of default—A formal, written notice to the borrower that a default has occurred and that legal action may take place.

Lien- A judgment against the property making it security for the payment

Prepayment penalty—A fee that may be charged to a borrower for paying off the loan before it is due.

Acceleration clause—A provision in a mortgage that gives the lender the right to demand payment of the entire outstanding balance of your mortgage loan.

There are different types of loans, financing programs (first-time homebuyers program, down payment assistance, etc.), and interest rates available to you. Do your research.

Step three: Find a realtor.

Find a realtor to assist you in the process of purchasing your home, especially if this is your first time. There are laws that you may not be aware of that, without proper understanding, may have you tangled in a web weaved so tightly it seems you could never get out.

I know you are thinking, *I don't want to pay a commission fee to a realtor just to help find a house. I can find one on my own.* Let me shine a light for you! The truth of the matter is you're not paying the commission fee; the realtor's commission is paid by the party who is selling their home.

The best way to choose your realtor is by word of mouth; ask around to see if someone can recommend a dependable realtor. Call different agencies until you find the right fit for you. One of my clients said that she chose me because she saw my picture in a real-estate magazine. She liked my picture because I had braids in my hair. Another client said that he was referred to me by a young lady to whom I had met and given my card at a home buying seminar. So you see, there are several different avenues you can take to find a realtor, and the process is easy. All you have to do is shop around until you find the right agent for you. It's important that you get the right person. You are going to be spending a lot of time with that person, so you really need to connect.

Step four: Find the perfect home.

Now that you are pre-approved and have a good realtor, it's time to sit down with your realtor to strategize your plan of attack that help you find the perfect home for you and your family.

To better prepare your realtor for the search for your new home, here is a list of general questions that your realtor will need your help to answer!

- What kind of house are you looking for? (For example, do you want a new or existing home, a condo, a townhouse, a two-story home, a split level, a mobile home, or a single-family one-story, ranch-style home?)
- Is there a particular area in which you are interested in living?
- What size home (minimum square-footage) are you looking for?
- How many bedrooms?
- How many baths?
- Do you want a garage? If so, a single or a double garage?
- Specific features

You really need to have a clear idea of what kind of home you are looking for; the clearer you are about what you want, the better the odds that your realtor can make it happen for you. If you don't know what you want, then how do you expect your realtor to know?

Once your realtor has a clear and concise understanding of what you are looking for, along with your pre-approval amount and the area (neighborhood) in which you are interested in purchasing your home, he or she will research that particular area to find the perfect match for you. Do not get upset if your realtor does not find any properties that match your criteria the first time searching. Houses are put on and taken off the market every day.

Keep this in mind: your realtor is the professional. So if after searching the system for your future home he or she comes back and tells you that you can't get a four-bedroom, two-bath home in the area you requested and for the price you would like, then please be flexible and allow your realtor to show you what's available in your price range in that area.

Your realtor may even suggest that you broaden your search area, which may allow you to get what you are seeking but in a different location of town. Sometimes when you are adamant about the area in which you wish to live, you narrow your chances of getting exactly what you want unless you have the funds and are willing to pay the price.

Once your realtor has found the perfect match for you and your family, it's time to take it to the next step! Now that you have signed your contract, made an offer (possibly even a counter offer), set your closing date, and have given your realtor your earnest money (escrow money), now it's time to get the ball rolling, which leads to our final steps.

Step five: Have the house inspected.

Congratulations! You have made it through half the process, and the reality of becoming a homeowner is only a few steps away! Don't give up now—you are almost home, girlfriend! Remember that I've got your back, and most importantly, "You can do all things through Christ Jesus, who strengthens you!" But I do want you to take a deep breath, because this is where the fun begins! It's inspection time. Once the contract and addendums are signed and agreed upon by both parties, you have a legal binding contract, also called an "executed contract." In most cases you have ten days to get through all of your home inspections, along with getting the property appraised. Check with your realtor to verify the amount of days allowed. It may vary from state to state.

There are several inspections that you may have to do, depending on the type of loan you have. It is to your benefit to make sure that you have all of the required inspections completed. Normally the buyer is responsible for the inspections, and the seller is responsible for a good, clean title and the search to prove that there are no liens on the property. The owner is the party selling the home.

Nuggets of Information

Verify with your realtor and your loan officer what inspections need to be performed before closing to complete your loan. This list may not be complete depending on your state or loan:

- Appraisal—normally paid by the buyer
- Title search—normally requested to be paid by the seller
- Repairs prior to close—normally paid by the seller up to set dollar or percent
- Survey—normally paid by the buyer
- Termite inspection—normally paid by the buyer
- Homeowners insurance—normally paid by the buyer
- Title insurance—normally paid by the buyer
- Flood insurance—normally paid by the buyer

Quick Reference Guide

Appraisal—an estimate of the value of the property; the act or process of estimating value.

Title search—an examination of the public records to determine the ownership and encumbrances affecting real property to verify that the property is lien-free and that the party selling the property is indeed the owner.

Survey—the process by which a parcel of land is measured and its area ascertained; it shows the measurements, boundaries, area, and contours of the property. This is done to confirm that the property boundaries are what is stated in the contract or purchase agreement.

Homeowners insurance—a policy designed to protect the owner from losses caused by theft and most common disasters.

Title insurance—an insurance policy that protects the holder from loss sustained by defects in the title. There are two types of polices: a lender's policy and an owner's policy. The owner's protects the owner and lender's policy protects the lender against defects.

Flood insurance—insurance that compensates for physical property in the event of a flood. Flood insurance is only required for properties that are in a federally designated flood area.

Hazard insurance—insurance that protects the lender and you against loss due to windstorm, fire, and natural disasters (hazard).

There may be other requirements that are not mentioned; check with your realtor and your loan officer!

You are not alone—I am still here! You are doing great! Take a deep breath. You are so close to achieving the American dream. Don't give up on me now. Remember, this is for you and your baby boy, too! He needs to see that you can do this, and he will be encouraged do the same, too!

Step six: Check the details.

Make sure that your lender has all of the necessary documents to make this deal happen. Double-check with your loan officer about all of the documents that need your signature, or any other documents that you need to provide to enable the loan to be closed.

Make sure that your rate is locked in to guarantee the interest rate that was offered to you. Generally speaking, your loan officer should have provided you with an estimate of what it would take you to close on your home. This is called a "good faith estimate." You should have received your estimate within three days of your application.

Quick Reference Guide

Lock-in—a written agreement guaranteeing the home buyer a specified interest rate, provided the loan closes within the set time.

Closing cost—expenses incurred by the buyer and the seller in transferring ownership of a property.

Settlement costs—See *Closing cost*, above.

Truth in Lending Act—a federal law that requires lenders to fully disclose, in writing, the terms and conditions of the mortgage, including the APR and/or other changes.

Points—a one-time charge by the lender to increase the yield of the loan to the current market interest rate. A point is 1 percent of the amount of the mortgage.

Prepaids—fees that are collected for setting up escrow accounts for property taxes, homeowner's insurance, and mortgage insurance.

PITI—the make-up of a monthly mortgage payment, which is the principal, interest, taxes, and insurance.

Principal—the amount owed on a debt, the borrowed amount, or the remaining unpaid amount on a loan.

Mortgage Insurance—a policy that protects the lender in the event of default by the mortgagor by guaranteeing repayment if the mortgagor dies.

The following is a list of just some of the documents needed in order for your loan officer to properly service your loan application:

- Your contract for the purchase
- Your banking information and statements
- Pay stubs, W-2 forms for the past two years, or proof of employment and salary (self-employed, loss and profit statement for the year to date, balance sheets, tax returns for the past two years)
- Information on all debt
- Information on your mortgage or rental payments, etc.

Your loan officer should have received all of the necessary documents prior to you finding your home or within the time given in the contract. Once all of the conditions have been met for your loan and you have the commitment letter from the lender, along with your signed sales contract, you are obligated to that contract, and so is the seller. This is the wrong time to get cold feet!

Step seven: Closing.

Finally the time has come for you to close. You are closer than ever to your dream of becoming a new homeowner, but we can't forget about your final walk-through inspection. Yes, one more inspection! But what did I say before about inspections? You are so right! You can only benefit from them!

Both you and your realtor should walk through the premises of your new home within twenty-four hours prior to closing to make sure that the sellers has vacated the premises and to check the property to make sure that all of the conditions stated in the contract have been met. It's also a good idea to make sure that the plumbing, electrical, heating, air-conditioning, and appliances all are working.

If conditions are not met or items not working, then it should be noted on your final walk-through form provided by your real-estate agent/realtor. You also need to initial the working items and most likely sign the form as well.

If you find major problems or violations of your contract concerning the condition of the property at the time of your walk-through, you have the right to postpone the closing until they are corrected or deduct the amount of money that it would take for the corrections of the problems or continue with the closing and have the items fixed after the closing. Some lending institution will not allow you to close if there are items still outstanding that need to be repaired.

Items in the house that you should make sure are in good, working condition:

- Heating system and equipment
- Air-conditioning unit and equipment

- Electrical system
- Plumbing equipment
- Oven and heating range
- Refrigerator
- Disposal
- Dishwasher
- Washer and dryer
- Pool and equipment
- Other items stated in the contract as part of the deal

The list provided is general information and may not be complete; please check with your realtor for assistance with a complete checklist at the time of your walk-through.

No! We are not there yet! But the good thing is we are less than a mile away from closing! If you look hard enough down the road, you can see your new home standing there waiting for you to occupy it. So it's time for you to take off those high heels and strap on your work boots, because it's going to get "a little hot in here," or, in other words, a little tough! But here's the key and the secret to all of what you may go through during this time: you can do all things through Christ Jesus, who strengthens you! I know I have repeated this several times. That's because I believe it, and I trust God even when I don't trust myself! Ladies, stand on his word and his promise!

Anything worth having requires hard work. Even relationships require work. Why do you think I wrote this book? It's all about the work required to relate to our young men and to help them relate in society! Blessed be God!

Now that you are knee-deep but stepping high, it's time to move on to the final phase of purchasing your new home. Your loan officer should provide you with the final figures from the HUD-1 (settlement statement) provided by the title company at least one day prior to your closing date. I have even seen it provided on the day of closing, so don't get discouraged if this happens. No personal checks are accepted—even though we know that your checks are good and won't bounce from sea to shining sea, because, girlfriend, you got it going on! But a certified check or a cashier's check will do! Normally what's included in the amount of your certified or cashier's check is the remainder of your closing cost (minus your escrow deposit/prepaid) and fees. The settlement statement helps to eliminate you (the buyer) from being hit with an unexpected dollar amount at the closing table.

Today is the big day, and you finally get to walk down that aisle. You have on your Sunday best looking good with your nice heels on! It's time for you to do that dance! It's the day of your closing! Congratulations, you have run the race and made it to the finish line! I know it feels good having someone on the sideline cheering you on! That would be *me*! That's right; you have your own personal fan club!

The closing is like a formal dinner party. Everybody sits around the table quietly, on their best behavior, nervously whispering and making idle chit-chat! It almost feels like you are on a first date. The atmosphere is a little awkward and stiff! But keep a smile on your face, because this is only the beginning of what's to be! Now you see that dreams can come true, but it's all up to you. Do you continue wishing upon a star, or will you finally wake up and put your life in gear by getting in the driver's seat of your life's little car? I know! I know! Corny!

OK, you are at the closing table, and it's time to sign the various documents. This part of the process may be very intimidating, so, go in expecting to sign at least fifty or more different documents. But before you sign on the dotted line, your closing agent should explain every form and document to you. If you don't understand what's being stated, stop your agent and asked him or her to explain it to you over again. This is a very important part of the process, so you really do want to know every little detail, because those documents are legal and binding!

Remember, it's OK to stop the closing agent and ask him or her to please go over that section again, or any section that you are unclear on.

Your closing agent has probably been closing loans for years and knows this information like the back of his or her hand. So he or she may be on cruise control when going over the documents and may take for granted that you know the information, too. Don't get yourself in tangled in a web because you missed out on some very important information, so be prepared for this process.

Nuggets of Information

- The lender has partial ownership until the loan is fully repaid (which is called an encumbrance), even though you have possession of the house. The mortgage simply restates the information stated in the note—the date of final payment, information on payment of PITI, information on hazard insurance, etc.—and it goes over maintaining the property. The mortgage goes over the basic items that are found in the note.
- In some states the mortgage is called the "deed of trust."
- The closing agent will go over the various costs to close with you and the seller. There are several different fees paid, such as the loan origination fee, the appraisal fee, the credit report fee, the loan discount point fee, the advance mortgage fee, the assumption fee (only when you take over the payments on the seller's existing loan), the mortgage insurance premium, advance payment/prepaid, interest, title charges, recording and recording fees, escrow accounts or reserves, the hazard insurance premium, the survey, and the test for termites. There could be additional charges and adjustments.

- The closing agent will also go over the bottom line, or, as some may call it, the "final reckoning" of the settlement statement/HUD-1.
- After all of the papers have been signed and the fees paid—every i dotted and t crossed—you are finally able to get the keys to your new home. Girlfriend, I am so proud of you!

Quick Reference Guide

Advance payments or prepaids—items paid before closing.

Appraisal fee—a fee paid for the appraisal.

Assumption fee—a fee paid to take over the payment on the seller's existing loan.

Credit report fee—a fee paid for pulling the borrower's credit report.

Hazard insurance premium—You may have to pay a one-year premium or bring proof to closing that you have it.

Loan discount points—a fee paid for the lender to adjust the yield on the loan to market conditions.

Loan origination fee—fees charged to cover the administration fee for processing the loan.

Recording and transfer fee—tax on the transfer of the property, required for recording the purchase.

Title charge—charges payable to companies or persons other than the lender, such as attorney's fees, title search fees, title insurance premium, and closing fees.

The first phase of your new life has just begun. This book was written for our young men, but for their mothers too. The next section of this book is dedicated to you, my sister. I want to drop some information in your ear to help secure your future. I am no expert and don't know all the answers, but a little knowledge will take you a long way! This area is very broad and requires an expert's attention, but I want to share with you the little information that I have on this subject! Make sure that you share this section with our boys, too! How you live now will affect how you live later, in your retirement.

Proverbs 24:5 (NLT)
A wise man is mightier than a strong man, and a man of knowledge is more powerful than a strong man.

CHAPTER 19

STOCKS, INVESTMENTS, and RETIREMENT

Planning is very important to your immediate life, future and retirement. You must plan for the future and rainy days or all of your days maybe a little stormy.

This subject can be very intimidating to most people; therefore, we tend to stay far away from it. Ladies, it's all about building a solid future, and the best way to begin is to lay one brick down at a time.

Wow! Where do I start? I have so much to tell you. I'm getting excited just anticipating the outcome of your bright future! We need to keep things simple in order for you to get it done! But I need for you to think big and think about change! It's all about standing up and facing the challenge. It's time to establish a safety net to help secure your future and your golden years.

When we are young, we tend to think that retirement is far, far away! You may also think that it's OK for you to wait until you get into your thirties before starting to save up for your retirement. I am here to tell you that's a big mistake! The earlier you start the better off you will be in twenty to twenty-five years when the thought of retirement seeps into the picture. You start thinking about how you can retire and live comfortably. Even though most large companies offer retirement plans, they are scaling way back, and now the burden is on you to save for your future, because of cutbacks. Uncle Sam is now saying that the younger generation (which may include you, depending on your age) may not even be able reap the benefits of social security because of the condition that it's now in. So, more than ever, we need to plan for our future. Don't look at the forest; concentrate on the trees! Look at your goals and not the length of time it's going to take to get to them. Sometimes the big picture can be overwhelming, so take a snapshot and hang on to it until you are able to look at the panoramic view! Let's strive to keep an eye on the big picture while we begin with the small picture.

Change can be very manageable and easy if you allow it. We tend to make things more painful than they really are. I know you may be used to walking into the store and spending your entire paycheck because you have another one coming in two weeks. That's true, and it's also true that your birthdays roll around much faster after thirty, and before you know it, you are sixty-five years old with no retirement, no nest egg, and still working a job waiting for those two weeks to roll past to collect a paycheck, when you should be thinking about what day you can hold your retirement party. At age sixty-five, I can see myself settled down, enjoying my grandkids, sipping on a cool, refreshing drink beside my pool, and not punching a time clock because I planned accordingly for my future! Now that I have beaten you over the head, and dragged you through the mud, I must help wash you off, clean your wounds, and help you put on some nice, clean bandages.

First let's place our foot on the brakes and put our car in park, because we need to establish some directions, or a safe route, to our new destination. There is no getting around it if you want to afford to live a secure life in the future. The hardest part of putting your future finances in shape is getting started. Remember, change is part of life, and no one can avoid change, no matter how we try. Our lives change every day, and we don't realize it. Every hour, every minute, every second, a change is taking place in our lives—it's called the aging process! You have no control over it, but you do have control over how you handle and prepare for it! Ladies, hear me and feel my heart. I want to see you sitting back at sixty-five or even seventy, sipping on a cool, refreshing soft drink, with your legs kicked up and your hands folded behind your head! So here's the plan. First, we need to take a close look at the available options you may have to help set in motion your retirement plan. There's no way to predict life's ups and downs, but it's important to be prepared for them, just in case!

Proverbs 24: 16a
For a just man falleth seven times, and riseth up again.

Here we go! I am still here with you and for you. You still have your support system in place, and remember, "You can do all things through Christ Jesus, who strengthens you!"

There are different stages in life, and you are growing mentally, physically, and socially throughout those stages. Things that matter in your twenties really don't matter so much in your forties. Just as life is lived in stages, we need to plan for our future in stages, because certain things are more important in certain stages. For instance, in your twenties and thirties you should consider the following.

- Increase your auto liability protection.
- Insure your possessions for replacement value.
- Check on your coverage, such as disability and life insurance, and consider a low-cost term life policy.

- Look at the amount you are paying for car insurance because of the car you are driving. The more expensive the car, the more you will pay to insure it! Consider buying a less expensive but dependable car.

Do you remember the huge mistake I made that I discussed in chapter 15? I wanted a Nissan Maxima so badly; I didn't care how I got it! The day I drove off the lot with my brand-new car, my heart was overjoyed with happiness. Six months later, when the honeymoon was over but the payments were not, things got old quickly! I was paying much more for my insurance because my vehicle was leased. It was a new vehicle with a hefty payment attached to it, but by the grace of God I have managed to pay my note every month! So, learn from my mistakes, or my trials and errors! The more you pay for the car, the higher your insurance premiums, and if you lease a vehicle, you have to take the highest limits available, which means, you will be paying higher premiums for leasing also.

As you age, you should readjust your policies according to your need. I am talking about all policies; even your health policies may need to be fine-tuned. Our needs change as our lives change. We should always go with the flow of things. Don't let the thought of this get you upset, thinking that every year you have to make changes. It's only necessary to change if there are major changes in your life. For example, a new child being born may require you to look at your health insurance and your life insurance policies. If you are in a financial rut, then you may want to consider temporarily adjusting the amount that you are having withheld from each paycheck and put into your savings or 401(k) accounts. Don't stop the deduction; just lower the amount that you have allotted to come out of your check.

Remember, our lives are constantly changing! Your needs are different once you hit ages forty and fifty. You have to think about illness, loss of income, and possible death of a significant other. You may be placed in a situation of having to be a caregiver to a parent or you may need a caregiver. Here are some things that you may need to consider at this stage in life:

You need to reassess your coverage again! Look at your homeowner's policy.

Consider

Cash-value life policies such as a cancer policy, accident, hospitalization, and critical illness policies
Benefit: Help in case a financial emergency arises, you are able to pull money from the policy to assist with your financial needs.

Disabilities policies
Benefit: Provide income in the event you are unable to work and earn money to provide for your household. Long term disability offers you a portion of your salary.

An umbrella policy
Benefit: Covers a much higher limit and goes above and beyond claims directly relating to your home and auto; protects your assets from unforeseen event such as a tragic accident in which you are held responsible for damages or bodily injuries.

Long-term care policies
Benefit: LTC policies provide coverage for nursing-home care, home health care, personal or adult day care for chronic or disabling conditions.

Keep an eye on your retirement plan
Benefit: Allows for any adjustments that may be needed to keep you on target for retirement and your golden years.

Review your estate plan
Benefit: Makes life easier for you and your family.

Types of Life Insurance

(Consult with a license Insurance Agent to assist with your decisions on which policy would fit your family needs)

Term life: The simplest form of life insurance, in which an insurer agrees to pay a certain death benefit if you die during the policy period. There are several types, including annual-renewable and level-premium term.

Annual-renewable: Term life insurance that is renewed each year. Normally the premiums increase each year as well.

Level-premium term insurance: Term life insurance on which premiums are projected or guaranteed level for a certain period, normally five, ten, fifteen, or twenty years.

Cash value life policies: Life insurance coverage that incorporates a tax-deferred savings component in addition to providing certain death benefits. The different types of cash value life policies are whole life, universal life, and variable life.

Whole life: The most widely purchased type of cash-valued life insurance. The coverage is usually guaranteed for the whole of the insured's life as long as the premiums are paid.

Universal life: A type of cash value life insurance that gives policyholders flexibility to skip payments or vary the amount they pay.

Disability insurance: Insurance that can replace part of your income if illness or injury leaves you unable to work for an extended amount of time.

Umbrella liability coverage: Supplemental liability insurance protection against lawsuits or other legal responsibilities.

Replacement value: The type of home insurance that pays the cost to replace or repair the home or possessions, up to the policy's set maximum. This type of coverage provides more protection than market-value coverage on the home or actual cash value coverage on contents.

Remember, it's all about planning for a better situation and better life, take your life in your hands by researching which policies are best for you and stay on top of your savings and retirement. Don't forget to consult a license professional to assist with determining what is best for you and your family! Making the right decision will allow you to plant your feet firmly on solid grounds and build a brighter future!

Proverbs 15:2a
The wise person makes learning a joy.

Single women are doing it and doing it well! Being a single parent isn't the ideal position to be in, but if you find yourself single and raising a child you still can achieve your goals and assist him in achieving his goals. There is no reason why you both can't win in life! Single mother's I salute your bravery in this journey and I stand beside you to encourage you on! Raising a boy to become a successful, healthy and productive man can be done with love, determination, and hard work!!

BOOKS REFERENCES

Act Like a Success, Think Like a Success: Discovering Your Gift and the Way to Life's Riches
Steve Harvey
Published 9/9/14

Jump: Take the Leap of Faith to Achieve Your Life of Abundance
Steve Harvey
Published 9/19/2017

Restoring the Male Image: A Look From the Inside Out
Alex O Ellis
9/12/2012

From the Pit to the Palace
Patrice C. Washington
Published 2/7/2013

Real Money Answers for Men: The Ultimate Playbook for Financial Success
Patrice C. Washington
Published 10/7/2014

Real Money Answers for Every Woman: How to Win the Money Game With or Without a Man
Patrice C. Washington
Published 1/19/2016

The 9 Steps to Financial Freedom: Practical and Spiritual Steps So You Can Stop Worrying
Suze Orman
Published 5/2/2007

The Money Class: Learn to Create Your New American Dream
Suze Orman
Published 3/8/2011

The Total Money Makeover: Classic Edition: A Proven Plan for Financial Fitness
Dave Ramsey
Published 9/17/2013

The Little Book of Value Investing
Christopher H. Browne
Published 9/22/2006

Rich Dad Poor Dad: What the Rich Teach Their Kids About Money That the Poor Middle Class Do Not!
Robert T. Kiyosaki
Published 4/11/2017

The Conscious Parent: Transforming Ourselves, Empowering Our Children
Dr. Shefali Tsabary
Published 11/1/2010

Positive Parenting: An Essential Guide (The Positive Parent Series)
Rebecca Eanes
Published 06/7/2016

Strong Mothers, Strong Sons: Lessons Mothers need to Raise Extraordinary Men
Meg Meeker
Published 4/7/2015

Single Mom's Raising Sons: Preparing Boys to Be Men When There's No Man Around
Dana S Chisholm
Published 9/19/2006

Websites:

www.suzeorman.com
www.realmoneyanswers.com
www.daveramsey.com
www.creditkarma.com
www.freecreditreport.com
www.experian.com

Additional resources:

Local church and their ministries
Single ministry
Women ministry
Teen ministry
Men ministry

Printed in the United States
By Bookmasters